EBB AND FLOW

EBB AND FLOW

VOLUME 2. WATER IN THE SHADOW OF CONFLICT IN THE MIDDLE EAST AND NORTH AFRICA

Edoardo Borgomeo, Anders Jägerskog, Esha Zaveri, Jason Russ,
Amjad Khan, and Richard Damania

CONTENTS

BOXES

FIGURES

TABLES

ACKNOWLEDGMENTS

This report is a flagship publication of the World Bank's Sustainable Development Practice prepared by Edoardo Borgomeo (Water Resources Management Specialist), Anders Jägerskog (Senior Water Resources Management Specialist), Esha Zaveri (Water Economist), Jason Russ (Senior Economist), and Amjad Khan (Young Professional) under the guidance of Richard Damania (Chief Economist). Ai-Ju Huang (Senior Operations Officer), Amal Talbi (Lead Water Resources Management Specialist), Dominick de Waal (Senior Economist), Kamila Galeza (Social Development Specialist), Sally Zgheib (Senior Water Supply and Sanitation Specialist), Sarah Keener (Senior Social Development Specialist), and Talajeh Livani (Social Development Specialist) provided valuable contributions.

The report has greatly benefited from the strategic guidance and general direction of Juergen Voegele (Vice President, Sustainable Development Practice Group), Jennifer Sara (Global Director, Water Practice), Carmen Nonay (Practice Manager), Soma Ghosh Moulik (Practice Manager), and the management of the Water Global Practice and the Middle East and North Africa Region.

The report draws from a background paper prepared by Majd Al Naber, Reem Al Haddadin, Barik Mhadeen, Kareem al-Sharabi, and Lina AlHaj Ahmad of the WANA Institute, "Policy Analysis: Migration and Conflict in the Middle East and North Africa."

The team wishes to thank the report's peer reviewers and other colleagues who provided valuable, insightful comments during the review process: Amal Talbi (Lead Water Resources Management Specialist), Dilip Ratha (Lead Economist), Dorte Verner (Lead Agriculture Economist), Erika S. Weinthal (Professor, Duke University), Erwin De Nys (Lead Water Resources Management Specialist), Ethel Sennhauser (Director), Harun Onder (Senior Economist), Hoveida Nobakht (Practice Manager), Kanta Kumari Rigaud (Lead Environment Specialist), Nancy Lozano Gracia (Senior Economist), Nathan Engle (Senior Climate Change Specialist), Nicolas Salazar Godoy (Social Development Specialist), Olivier Lavinal (Senior Operations Officer), Pieter Waalewijn (Global Lead, Water for Agriculture), Somik Lall (Lead Urban Economist), Stavros (Aki) Stavrou (Senior Social Development Specialist), and Viviane Wei Chen Clement (Climate Change Specialist).

The report has also benefited from the comments, ideas, and data shared by academics and practitioners. The task team would like to thank Jeannie Sowers (University of New Hampshire), Michael Talhami (International Committee of the Red Cross), Neda A. Zawahri (Cleveland State University), Tobias Ide (University of Melbourne), and Stefan Döring (University of Uppsala).

Estelle Villemin and Francis Gagnon of Voilá Information Design provided skillful information design advice and designed the report's infographic.

The World Bank Water communications, knowledge, and publishing teams, particularly Erin Barrett, Meriem Gray, and Pascal Saura, provided valuable guidance for turning the manuscript into a finalized report. John Dawson provided excellent editorial support. Deborah Appel-Barker, Amy Lynn Grossman, Patricia Katayama, and Jewel McFadden from the World Bank's Publishing Program guided additional design, editing, and publication.

Finally, Georgine Badou provided helpful administrative support, for which the team is grateful.

This work was made possible by the financial contribution of the Global Water Security and Sanitation Partnership of the Water Global Practice, World Bank Group. For more information, go to www.worldbank.org/gwsp.

EXECUTIVE SUMMARY

When he first arrived in Jordan, Abd was shocked by the lack of water. He fled the Syrian Arab Republic in 2013 out of fear for his children's lives and the destruction of their house. Since arriving in Jordan, he has grown accustomed to conserving water and using less of it. "Water shortages are a constant risk," he said, "and with COVID-19, I have had to buy additional water from tankers at great cost for my family." Abd is one among millions across the Middle East and North Africa who are forcibly displaced and facing water insecurity.

With the region experiencing the highest levels of forced displacement in the world and growing water scarcity under climate change, countries increasingly contend with policy issues at the nexus of water, conflict, and forced displacement. An estimated 7.6 million refugees, around 2.7 million of whom are hosted in the region, and 12.4 million internally displaced persons (IDPs) are fleeing the region's protracted armed conflicts (both international and noninternational armed conflicts) (UNHCR 2020; IDMC and NRC 2020). The Middle East and North Africa is also the most water-scarce region in the world, with over 60 percent of its population living in areas with high water stress (World Bank 2017a). It also experiences some of the world's highest levels of interannual hydrological variability, meaning that it is exposed to both long droughts and devastating floods. And while the countries of the Middle East and North Africa have managed to significantly expand access to water services over the past three decades, these achievements are now challenged by groundwater depletion, urban expansion, governance issues, and conflict.

Ebb and Flow: Volume 2. Water in the Shadow of Conflict in the Middle East and North Africa examines the links between water risks (harmful outcomes related to water, from droughts and floods to lack of sanitation), conflict, and forced displacement. It aims to increase understanding of how to address the vulnerabilities of forcibly displaced persons and their host communities, and to identify water policies and investment responses. Building on the framework in figure ES.1 and findings presented in *Ebb and Flow: Volume 1. Water, Migration, and Development* (Zaveri et al. 2021)—

FIGURE ES.1: Framework to Examine the Interplay of Water, Conflict, and Forced Displacement in the Middle East and North Africa

Why	Who	Where and What
• Why and in what contexts does water contribute to conflict and forced displacement?	• Who are the forcibly displaced populations and their host communities?	• Where do the forcibly displaced populations live? • What water risks do they face?

Source: World Bank.

see summary in annex ES.A—this report tackles three key questions: (a) Why and in what contexts does water contribute to conflict and forced displacement? (b) Who are the forcibly displaced populations and their host communities? and (c) Where do forcibly displaced people live and what water risks do they face? To address these questions, the report uses statistical analysis of historical event databases, case studies based on semistructured interviews, and a review of the existing literature.

WHY AND IN WHAT CONTEXTS DOES WATER CONTRIBUTE TO CONFLICT AND FORCED DISPLACEMENT?

While some research suggests that there is a direct link between water, conflict, and forced displacement, the evidence suggests caution in invoking causal relationships. Particular caution is needed when considering claims that forced displacement is an intervening variable linking water risks with conflict, as suggested for the Syrian crisis. The context-specific nature of the water and displacement relationship holds a few overarching key insights. First, the relationship between water and forced displacement, especially large-scale displacement, is a complex one. While water risks can affect choices to move—as discussed in volume 1 of *Ebb and Flow*—the complexity of interacting factors influencing individual and household choices means that it is not possible to identify water migrants in the Middle East and North Africa. Second, there are local instances of forced displacement in response to water risks (notably lack of basic water services and drought), but this movement is mostly internal and not transnational. Third, research and analysis should focus on the effects that water and agricultural policy might have in exacerbating or mitigating the effects of water risks on vulnerable populations, their livelihoods, and income-generating activities rather than trying to identify "water migrants."

Historically, water has more frequently been associated with cooperation than conflict, at both the international and national levels. This report draws on well-known event databases of domestic water events—the Water-Related Intrastate Conflict and Cooperation data set (Bernauer et al. 2012)—and international water events—the Transboundary Freshwater Dispute Database of Oregon State University (Wolf 1998; De Stefano et al. 2010)—to build a historical picture of both cooperation and conflict in relation to water in the region. Analysis of historical events reveals that cooperation—ranging from verbal agreements over water sharing to construction of infrastructure—was the most frequent outcome arising from water-related issues in the Middle East and North Africa. This holds both for events related to domestic water issues and for international events, defined as events related to transboundary rivers and aquifers. Interestingly, this finding is confirmed when other key water-related constraints, such as challenging access to groundwater, are taken into account. In the Middle East and North Africa, water-scarce areas have been found to experience more instances of water cooperation, including in areas where groundwater is difficult to access (Döring 2020). This confirms evidence from other parts of the world suggesting that long-term exposure to water scarcity strengthens water users' preference for cooperation (Nie, Yang, and Tu 2020; Haseeb 2020). While clearly this does not exclude the possibility of water-related disputes in the future, it does suggest that research and policy should focus more on the potential role of water for building cooperation.

Although forced displacement and conflict are uncertain and indirect consequences of water risks, the reverse is a real and concerning outcome of conflict: water is increasingly a casualty and weapon of conflict (Sowers, Weinthal, and Zawahri 2017; Gleick 2019). Water infrastructure and services have even been targets in the conflicts in the region. In Syria, 457 water supply and sanitation assets have been damaged, which includes damage to or destruction of two-thirds of the country's water treatment plants and half of its pumping stations (World Bank 2017b). In addition, long-term effects of damages on water infrastructure in Gaza, Iraq, Libya, and the Republic of Yemen are also putting a heavy burden on those economies, severely hampering the possibilities for reconstruction. Targeting of water infrastructure is perhaps the most concerning trend identified in this report: since 2011, there have been 180 instances of targeting of water infrastructure in the region's conflicts in Libya, Syria, and the Republic of Yemen alone. (Sowers, Weinthal, and Zawahri 2017)

Climate change and soaring demand are adding pressure on economies and livelihoods dependent on already depleted and degraded water resources. This observation suggests that future water, forced displacement, and conflict dynamics might look very different from the historical patterns described in this report. As evidence of the disproportionate effects of climate change on countries and populations enduring conflict grows, so does the need to continue monitoring the dynamics described in this report in light of ever-changing conditions. In the Middle East and North Africa, decades of conflict have increased people's vulnerability to climate change. In places that lack strong governance and inclusive institutions, climate change might further exacerbate vulnerabilities and tensions over water resources, in a vicious cycle of water insecurity and fragility (Sadoff, Borgomeo, and De Waal 2017).

LEAST PROTECTED, MOST AFFECTED: WHO ARE THE FORCIBLY DISPLACED POPULATIONS, WHERE DO THEY LIVE, AND WHAT WATER RISKS DO THEY FACE?

Water is among the main factors determining the vulnerabilities of people who are forcibly displaced. Access to safe and affordable drinking water services remains a key humanitarian priority in both the short and medium term across the region. Forcibly displaced populations in countries and territories affected by protracted armed conflict (Gaza, Iraq, Libya, Syria, and the Republic of Yemen) all identify drinking water as one of their key priorities alongside food and shelter. Even when this immediate need is met, evidence suggests that displaced populations face additional challenges related to water safety and affordability. Access to adequate sanitation also remains a challenge for forcibly displaced persons in places of both origin and destination, with the exception of some Palestinian refugees in the West Bank and populations living in camps. Marginalized groups within forcibly displaced communities face additional challenges in accessing water services. In camps and host communities, measures to meet the needs of people with disabilities are often lacking. Furthermore, in situations of forced displacement, women and girls are most exposed to adversity, and many of the water risks they face are heightened. Women face a number of water risks, including higher rates of gender-based violence exacerbated by the inadequate access to water and sanitation facilities and the impacts of water shocks on livelihoods and well-being, for example through the effects on food production.

The COVID-19 pandemic has brought additional challenges affecting both affordability and availability of water. COVID-19 means that more water is needed in camps, informal settlements, and host communities to enable adequate handwashing and hygiene. In water-scarce areas with low service coverage where most forcibly displaced persons live, such as in informal settlements or remote refugee camps, these additional water requirements have translated into higher expenditure to fetch water from vendors. Those challenges, coupled with increased economic hardship, further underscore affordability issues. In Jordan, Syrian refugees reported a doubling of their expenses related to water, as they had to purchase more water from tankers and buy soap and hand sanitizers. In addition, water and sanitation facilities in camps and informal settlements are often shared, thereby heightening the risk of infection.

Forcibly displaced populations also face additional water resource risks relating to water scarcity and floods. In the Republic of Yemen, water scarcity is cited by IDPs and returnees as one of the main factors in the decline of their livelihoods and of access to income-generating activities. Increased availability of water for agriculture is one of the most frequently reported requirements for improved livelihoods by both IDPs and host communities. While there is no regionwide assessment of the flood risks faced by forcibly displaced persons, country evidence suggests that flooding is a key determinant of vulnerability. Refugee and IDP camps in Syria and the Republic of Yemen are at a particular risk of flooding, with tens of thousands of forcibly displaced persons having to relocate because of flooding in 2020 alone.

Forced displacement puts an unplanned burden on the water and related services of host communities. An estimated 80 to 90 percent of the forcibly displaced persons in the Middle East and North Africa live outside camps, in towns and cities (World Bank 2017c). This situation can compound difficulties that some cities are already facing in providing basic services, including drinking water supply and wastewater collection and treatment services. The sudden arrival of large numbers of forcibly displaced persons often causes severe stress on public services and environmental impacts on land, water, and other natural resources. The presence of forcibly displaced persons in host communities is also accelerating depletion of water resources and degrading water quality. These impacts mean that communities that host forcibly displaced persons have to increase their investments and ramp up their plans for increasing coverage of water supply and sanitation services and protecting water sources.

WATER: AN OPPORTUNITY TO BUILD RESILIENCE

The protracted nature of the forced displacement crisis in the Middle East and North Africa and increasing water scarcity call for a shift from humanitarian support toward long-term pathways for water security. There is an urgent need to develop and implement sustainable long-term solutions to enhance water security and build resilience to future shocks. This report puts forward an integrated framework for development actors to respond to water risks in situations of protracted forced displacement (figure ES.2).

The components of figure ES.2 should be understood as building blocks to enhance water security for forcibly displaced populations and their host communities in the Middle East and North Africa. In phases of development, people- and area-based interventions constitute the first building block toward

FIGURE ES.2: Approach for Development Actors to Promote Water Security for Forcibly Displaced People and Their Host Communities

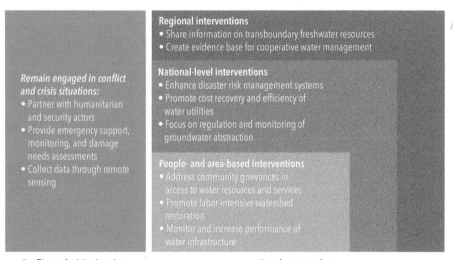

Regional interventions
- Share information on transboundary freshwater resources
- Create evidence base for cooperative water management

National-level interventions
- Enhance disaster risk management systems
- Promote cost recovery and efficiency of water utilities
- Focus on regulation and monitoring of groundwater abstraction

People- and area-based interventions
- Address community grievances in access to water resources and services
- Promote labor-intensive watershed restoration
- Monitor and increase performance of water infrastructure

Remain engaged in conflict and crisis situations:
- Partner with humanitarian and security actors
- Provide emergency support, monitoring, and damage needs assessments
- Collect data through remote sensing

Spatial scale

Conflict and crisis situations   Development phase

Source: World Bank.

water security. Policies to reconstruct national institutions and components of water resource management are likely to fail without the foundations of a renewed social fabric and trust in institutions, which can be achieved through people- and area-based interventions. People- and area-based approaches can help to address grievances and social inclusion barriers, notably gender gaps, related to access to water resources and services in protracted crisis situations.

In the water sector, people- and area-based interventions focus on ensuring access to water services and protecting livelihood opportunities supported by water. Public work programs to reverse the degradation of watersheds and other labor-intensive approaches to monitor, clean up, and restore degraded water resources enhance water's potential to support livelihoods. People-based interventions can also support activities to empower and build the skills of those who are responsible for water resource management and supplies within forcibly displaced and host communities.

People- and area-based interventions need to be aligned with investments in national-level institutions and infrastructure. These interventions aim at restoring the national-level building blocks that are essential to ensure sustainable water management and service delivery. Institutional interventions can focus on groundwater management and regulation, as well as giving attention to financial sustainability issues for water service providers. Expansion and rehabilitation of water infrastructure are key interventions to restore national building blocks for water security. These interventions will need to plan for potential targeting through, for example, redundancies (replicating elements of infrastructure, designing systems with diversified supply sources), contingency plans (stocking up consumables for water treatment plants, nominating replacement staff), and prioritization of easy-to-operate wastewater treatment solutions with minimal or no need for grid electricity (such as stabilization ponds and constructed wetlands). One example in which a positive development has taken place is in the Kurdistan region of Iraq, where water supply and sanitation coverage has slightly increased following the influx of refugees from Syria and IDPs from other parts of Iraq. This progress suggests that the region's government and its development partners adapted quickly to improve water supply, with indicators for coverage improving since the start of the Syrian crisis.

Finally, a political economy approach that considers a regional perspective complements the national-level and people- and area-based approaches. The Syrian conflict, for example, has led to a number of regional externalities, not just in terms of the tragic numbers of forcibly displaced people, but also in terms of a decrease in cross-border trade (World Bank 2020). These are examples of "public bads" that require regional and international coordination if they are to be overcome. Transboundary waters offer another example of cross-border flows and regional issues whose public good benefits can turn into public bads without a concerted effort by regional actors. Therefore, water sector interventions in response to protracted forced displacement need to consider regional issues and the

FIGURE ES.3: Decision Points in Response to Water Risks Faced by Forcibly Displaced People and Their Host Communities

Source: World Bank.

potential for coordinated cross-border responses through transboundary water cooperation.

When working toward the integrated approach shown in figure ES.2, policy makers will likely face trade-offs between short-term uncoordinated measures to respond to immediate water needs and long-term measures needed to address structural water sector issues. These trade-offs are time specific, meaning that they can create path dependencies and lock-in, thus influencing the ability of countries to achieve water security over the long term. Hence, at different stages of a protracted forced displacement crisis, policy makers need to be cognizant of the fact that their efforts can undermine or support long-term water security objectives, as shown in figure ES.3. The figure shows three decision points at which specific trade-offs shape which paths are taken: (1) prevention and pre-crisis coordination and planning, (2) the response to protracted forced displacement, and (3) preparation for recovery and return. Countries might end up in very different water security situations depending on the choices their leaders make at each of these points. Unless these trade-offs are recognized and managed, water risks are likely to undermine progress toward recovery and sustainable peace, in a vicious cycle of water insecurity and fragility. The intersection of water resources, conflict, and forced displacement in the Middle East and North Africa is summarized in figure ES.4.

To conclude, this report suggests that rather than trying to unpack complex causal linkages between water, forced displacement, and conflict, development policy and analysis should focus on designing interventions to address the water risks faced by forcibly displaced people and host communities now and in the future. Looking ahead, water has the potential to enable post-conflict reconstruction and cooperation efforts. To capture this potential, water interventions need to promote (1) close coordination between all actors (security, humanitarian and development) and (2) trust in institutions and a renewed social fabric, which can be achieved through people- and area-based water sector interventions.

WATER IN THE SHADOW OF CONFLICT

Given the **unprecedented levels** of forced displacement and conflict in the **Middle East and North Africa (MENA)**, water policy needs to address the vulnerabilities of the forcibly displaced people and host communities. Water can exacerbate risks of conflict and forced displacement, but it can also create **opportunities for cooperation.**

1 THE COLLISION OF WATER SCARCITY, CONFLICT AND FORCED DISPLACEMENT is UNPRECEDENTED

2 WATER CAN BE A SOURCE OF CONFLICT... OR COOPERATION

Historically water has more often led to cooperation than conflict. However, the **relationship between water, conflict, and cooperation** may change in the future.

An estimated **7.6 million** refugees, around 2.7 million of whom are hosted in the region, and

12.4 million internally displaced people are fleeing the region's protracted armed conflicts.

1 person out of 4 in Lebanon is a refugee.

WATER IS A VICTIM OF CONFLICT

Infrastructure targeting: 180 instances of intentional targeting of water infrastructure in Libya, the Syrian Arab Republic, and the Republic of Yemen since 2011.

70% of MENA's GDP is generated in areas with **high or very high water stress** compared to 22% in the rest of the world.

WATER IS A WEAPON OF CONFLICT

Armed groups take control of water infrastructure to threaten opponents and deliver basic water services to delegitimize state and complicate peacebuilding efforts.

Population living in areas with **high water stress:**

Rest of the world	MENA region
35%	60%

INTERNATIONAL

Out of the 975 water-related events recorded in the region, most are **cooperative.**

37% 56%
8%

DOMESTIC

Out of 1,317 water-related events recorded in the region, most were **cooperative** or neutral.

19% 33%
48%

Cooperative
Neutral
Conflictive

Source: World Bank.

WATER is A DAILY STRUGGLE FOR FORCIBLY DISPLACED PEOPLE AND THEIR HOST COMMUNITIES

IN HOST COMMUNITIES

64% of Syrians in Jordan are **highly vulnerable** to water and sanitation risk.

In 50% of Libya's **municipalities,** forcibly displaced people find water to to be **unaffordable.**

Demand for water since the arrival of **Syrian refugees in 2012:**

+40% Northern governates of Jordan
+30% Northern Iraq
+20% Lebanon

2012   2020

IN CONFLICT-AFFECTED AREAS

In the Republic of Yemen, **2 out of 3** forcibly displaced people do not have access to **a safe and functioning latrine.**

25% of displaced people inside the Syrian Arab Republic **share sanitation facilities** with at least **6 people.**

In the Republic of Yemen, **18 million people** do not have access to **safe drinking water supplies.**

1 in 4 international migrant in Libya does not have **enough water to drink.**

IN CAMPS AND INFORMAL SETTLEMENTS

In Jordan, households with **disability** report **lower rates of access** to sanitation services.

At least **a quarter of all Syrian refugee households** in informal settlements in Lebanon are accessing very **highly contaminated drinking water.**

Every year, **flash flooding** inflicts extensive **damage** to camps and informal settlements.

I am very concerned that water shortage will happen in Jordan. Since I arrived in Mafraq water cuts have happened constantly.

Rama, Syrian refugee in Jordan

Water from the camp's taps is too salty to drink, especially in the summer.

Mohammad, Palestinian refugee in Lebanon

COVID-19 has caused water shortages here, and now we have to buy more expensive water from water tankers.

Samar, Syrian refugee in Jordan

ANNEX ES.A: MAIN FINDINGS FROM *EBB AND FLOW: VOLUME 1*

Ebb and Flow: Volume 1. Water, Migration, and Development (Zaveri et al. 2021) examines the effect of water shocks (defined as rainfall that is at least 1 standard deviation below or above long-term averages) on internal migration and finds that cumulative dry water shocks play a significant role in influencing migration, with water deficits resulting in five times as much migration as water excess. Internal migration responses to water differ systematically between low-income and middle-income settings. Where there is extreme poverty and migration is costly, water deficits are more likely to trap people than induce them to migrate. Water shocks affect not only the number of people who move, but also the skills they bring with them. For example, workers who leave regions because of water deficits tend to be lower skilled. Cities are the destination of most internal migrants, yet even in cities water scarcity can haunt them. Depending on the size of the water shock, city growth can slow by up to 12 percent during a water deficit, enough to reverse critical development progress.

REFERENCES

Bernauer, T., T. Böhmelt, H. Buhaug, N. P. Gleditsch, T. Tribaldos, E. B. Weibust, and G. Wischnath. 2012. "Water-Related Intrastate Conflict and Cooperation (WARICC): A New Event Dataset." *International Interactions: Empirical and Theoretical Research in International Relations* 38 (4): 529–45.

De Stefano, L., P. Edwards, L. De Silva, and A. T. Wolf. 2010. "Tracking Cooperation and Conflict in International Basins: Historic and Recent Trends." *Water Policy* 12 (6): 871-884.

Döring, S. 2020. "From Bullets to Boreholes: A Disaggregated Analysis of Domestic Water Cooperation in Drought-Prone Regions." *Global Environmental Change* 65: 102147.

Gleick, P. H. 2019. "Water as a Weapon and Casualty of Armed Conflict: A Review of Recent Water-Related Violence in Iraq, Syria, and Yemen." *Wiley Interdisciplinary Reviews: Water* 6 (4): e1351.

Haseeb, M. 2020. *Resources Scarcity and Cooperation: Job Market Paper*. https://warwick.ac.uk/fac/soc/economics/staff/mhaseeb/jmp_haseeb.pdf.

IDMC and NRC (Internal Displacement Monitoring Centre and Norwegian Refugee Council). 2020. *Global Report on Internal Displacement*. Geneva: IDMC. https://www.internal-displacement.org/sites/default/files/publications/documents/2019-IDMC-GRID.pdf.

Nie, Z., X. Yang, and Q. Tu. 2020. "Resource Scarcity and Cooperation: Evidence from a Gravity Irrigation System in China." *World Development* 135: 105035.

Sadoff, C. W., E. Borgomeo, and D. De Waal. 2017. *Turbulent Waters: Pursuing Water Security in Fragile Contexts*. Washington, DC: World Bank.

Sowers, J. L., E. Weinthal, and N. Zawahri. 2017. "Targeting Environmental Infrastructures, International Law, and Civilians in the New Middle Eastern Wars." *Security Dialogue* 48 (5): 410–30.

UNHCR (United Nations High Commissioner for Refugees). 2020. *Global Trends: Forced Displacement in 2019*. Geneva: UNHCR. https://www.unhcr .org/5ee200e37.pdf.

Wolf, A. 1998. "Conflict and Cooperation along International Waterways." *Water Policy* 1 (2): 251–65.

World Bank. 2017a. *Beyond Scarcity: Water Security in the Middle East and North Africa*. Middle East and North Africa Development Report. Washington, DC: World Bank.

World Bank. 2017b. *The Toll of War: The Economic and Social Consequences of the Conflict in Syria*. Washington, DC: World Bank.

World Bank. 2017c. *Cities of Refuge in the Middle East: Bringing an Urban Lens to the Forced Displacement Challenge*. Washington, DC: World Bank.

World Bank. 2020. *The Fallout of War: The Regional Consequences of the Conflict in Syria*. Washington, DC: World Bank.

Zaveri, Esha, Jason Russ, Amjad Khan, Richard Damania, Edoardo Borgomeo, and Anders Jägerskog. 2021. *Ebb and Flow: Volume 1. Water, Migration, and Development*. Washington, DC: World Bank.

ABBREVIATIONS

COVID-19   coronavirus
FAO   Food and Agriculture Organization of the United Nations
GDP   gross domestic product
ICRC   International Committee of the Red Cross
IDP   internally displaced person
UNHCR   United Nations High Commissioner for Refugees
UNICEF   United Nations Children's Fund
UNRWA   United Nations Relief and Works Agency for Palestine
                Refugees in the Near East
WARICC   water-related intrastate conflict and cooperation
WHO   World Health Organization

CHAPTER ONE

THE UNPRECEDENTED COLLISION OF WATER SCARCITY, CONFLICT, AND FORCED DISPLACEMENT

No one leaves home unless
Home is the mouth of the shark

You only run for the border
When you see the whole city running as well
Your neighbors running faster than you
Breath bloody in their throats
. . . . . .
You only leave home
When home won't let you stay

— Warsan Shire, "Home"

KEY HIGHLIGHTS

- The Middle East and North Africa region is witnessing the collision of climate change, soaring water demands, and weak water governance, with unprecedented levels of protracted forced displacement and conflict.

- Given the unprecedented levels of forced displacement and the protracted nature of conflicts in the Middle East and North Africa, water policy and investment need to increasingly address the vulnerabilities of forcibly displaced populations and their host communities.

- This report examines evidence on the links between water risks, forced displacement, and conflict using statistical analysis of historical event databases, case studies based on semistructured interviews, and a review of existing literature.

INTRODUCTION

The Middle East and North Africa region encapsulates many of the issues surrounding water and human mobility. It is the most water-scarce region in the world, with more than 60 percent of its population living in areas with high water stress (World Bank 2017a). The region is a global hot spot of water resource depletion, with surface and groundwater resources being exploited beyond their natural replenishment rates (Borgomeo et al. 2020). Water quality is also declining, with more than 57 percent of the region's wastewater being discharged untreated into surface water bodies (World Bank 2017a). It also experiences some of world's highest levels of interannual hydrological variability, meaning that it is exposed to both long droughts and devastating floods. In addition, about 60 percent of surface water resources in the region are transboundary, and every country in the Middle East and North Africa shares at least one aquifer with a neighbor (World Bank 2017a). Climate change and population growth further exacerbate these challenges (box 1.1). The challenges are not just related to water, of course: the region is characterized by socioeconomic and political fragmentation, high unemployment, and a broken social contract (Devarajan and Ianchovichina 2018; Elitok and Fröhlich 2019).

Historically, the region has also experienced high levels of intraregional and international human mobility and, more recently, unprecedented levels of forced displacement. As of 2020, there were an estimated 7.6 million refugees and asylum seekers, of whom about 2.7 million were hosted in the region, and 12.4 million internally displaced persons (IDPs) fleeing the region's protracted armed conflicts (both international and noninternational armed conflicts) (UNHCR 2020; IDMC 2020; IDMC and NRC 2020) (see appendix A for definitions).

BOX 1.1: Climate Change, Population Growth, and the Middle East and North Africa's Water Crisis

The collision of population growth and climate change makes the Middle East and North Africa's water issues a more urgent challenge than ever before. Many countries in the region, particularly those affected by conflict and forced displacement, are already eroding their water resource base through water overuse and pollution. About half of the region's water use is unsustainable, meaning that water is being used faster than it is naturally being replenished. Depletion has already resulted in groundwater wells and rivers running dry, especially in countries facing fragility and conflict such as Iraq, Libya, Syrian Arab Republic, and the Republic of Yemen. Beyond overuse, pollution is also a major issue, with at least 50 percent of the region's wastewater being returned untreated into the environment.

Although access to water supply and sanitation services has improved in recent decades, access levels are declining in countries affected by fragility and conflict. Very large disparities exist in terms of the quality and reliability of water services within countries, particularly in terms of rural–urban gaps, which are particularly stark in Iraq, Morocco, and the Republic of Yemen. Poorer households, often located in areas unserved by utilities, have to buy poor-quality water from water vendors at prices much higher than those paid by users connected to piped water supplies. Inadequate water supply and sanitation cost about 1 percent of regional gross domestic product (GDP) annually, with conflict-affected countries losing as much as 2–4 percent annually. In these countries, mortality due to unsafe water supply and sanitation is also greater than global averages.

Climate change is already happening in the region and is further exacerbating water-sector issues. Key observed impacts include loss of winter precipitation and declining snow storage inducing summer droughts, less frequent and more intense rainfall events causing droughts and flash floods, and higher temperatures and heat waves leading to increasing agricultural water demand and strained livelihoods and ecosystems. The region has the greatest expected economic losses from climate-related water scarcity, estimated at 6–14 percent of GDP by 2050. Increased surface water stress due to climate change will occur in countries facing politically and environmentally fragile situations. Projections suggest that Iraq, Jordan, Lebanon, and Syria will all experience significantly increased water stress driven by climate change.

Sources: Verner 2012; World Bank 2017a.

The region's human mobility story can be broadly characterized by three interlinked patterns. First and foremost, forced displacement occurs as a result of protracted armed conflict and violence. The conflict in the Syrian Arab Republic has led to the largest forced displacement crisis in the world, including significant numbers of IDPs as well as refugees. Syria recently overtook Afghanistan as the country of origin of most refugees in the world (World Bank 2017c; World Bank 2020). In addition to Syria, forced displacement is also prevalent in other countries, such as Iraq, Libya, and the Republic of Yemen, all of which still face situations of protracted armed conflict. While today the numbers of forcibly displaced persons in the region are at record levels, numbers of forcibly displaced persons have been high throughout its history. Some of the region's protracted armed conflicts (for example, the Israeli-Palestinian conflict, the Iraqi wars, the civil war in Lebanon, and disputes in Western Sahara) mean that forced displacement has been a long-term challenge in the Middle East and North Africa. In general, forced displacement is seen as being a result of wars, political unrest, ethnic oppression, food scarcity, natural disasters, and climate change (Swain and Jägerskog 2016). The levels of vulnerability of the groups that are forced to leave their homes are significant and are often the result of a combination of these factors. Since the first Arab-Israeli war in 1948, the region has been hosting more than 5.6 million Palestinian refugees (this is the number of Palestinian refugees under the mandate of the United Nations Relief and Works Agency). Similarly, the Kurdish population, spanning Iraq, the Islamic Republic of Iran, Syria, and Turkey, has been experiencing forced displacement at scale for decades (McDowall 1996).

The region's forced displacement situation is protracted, requiring a long-term view to respond to the many development challenges it poses. For example, surveys of Syrian refugees show that up to a quarter of them do not plan to return to their homes, suggesting that development policy will increasingly have to tackle their long-term needs and rights (UNHCR 2018). This is also consistent with the trend over the past decade worldwide. The United Nations High Commissioner for Refugees (UNHCR) notes that over the past decade, less than 4 million refugees were able to return compared with almost 10 million in the preceding decade and 15 million two decades prior. As conflicts tend to be more protracted, the forcibly displaced people in the region will be less likely to be able to return (UNHCR 2020).

The second pattern of the human mobility story of the Middle East and North Africa consists of the complex movements of people within and transiting the region. This movement is driven by a variety of factors, including a mix of economic and other factors. This second pattern falls under the complex phenomenon of migration, as described in *Ebb and Flow: Volume 1* (Zaveri et al. 2021). Some migrants move within the region, for example toward the Gulf countries,[1] while others pass through the region, mostly toward Europe. Although numbers are uncertain, North African countries alone hosted an estimated 2.9 million international migrants in 2019, of which about half were refugees and asylum seekers transiting the region toward Europe (UN DESA 2019; GMDAC 2021).

Finally, a third important dimension of the migration story in the Middle East and North Africa relates to labor migrants—from both within and outside the region—in the Gulf countries and, to a lesser extent, Jordan and Lebanon. In 2019, there were 35 million international migrants in the Gulf Cooperation Council countries and Jordan and Lebanon, of whom 31 percent were women (UN DESA 2019).

FOCUS OF THE REPORT

This report focuses on the first pattern of human mobility in the region, and seeks to understand the role of water in the forced displacement and conflict story of the Middle East and North Africa. Forcibly displaced persons are defined here as people who leave their homes because of force, compulsion, or coercion, typically because of violence and conflict (World Bank 2017b). This definition includes refugees, asylum seekers, and internally displaced persons. Although the main focus is on forcibly displaced people, the report also describes some of the links between water and the second migration pattern described above, consisting of the complex movements of international migrants within and transiting the region. When referring to this pattern, the report follows the International Organization for Migration's definition of "migrant" (see appendix A).

This report attempts to shed some light on the interplay of water risks, forced displacement, and conflict, and to inform development policy responses. *Water risks* are here interpreted as harmful outcomes related to water, such as flooding and drought, but also lack of access to safe drinking water and sanitation services. Statistical analysis of historical event databases, case studies based on semistructured interviews, and a review of existing literature are used to explore this issue. In examining the interplay between water, forced displacement, and conflict, the report does not try to provide definitive answers on the complex links between water risks and migration, or to produce regional estimates of water-related migration. Indeed, as noted elsewhere (Wrathall et al. 2018), caution is warranted when examining the links between water and human mobility, especially in contexts affected by protracted armed conflict. This report follows the framework for understanding water and human mobility laid out in volume 1 of *Ebb and Flow*, adapting it to the case of forced displacement in the Middle East and North Africa. The focus is on three questions of relevance for policy (figure 1.1):

1. Why and in what contexts does water contribute to conflict and forced displacement?

2. Who are the forcibly displaced populations and their host communities?

3. Where do forcibly displaced people live and what water risks do they face?

FIGURE 1.1: **Framework to Examine the Interplay of Water, Conflict, and Forced Displacement in the Middle East and North Africa**

Why	Who	Where and What
• Why and in what contexts does water contribute to conflict and forced displacement?	• Who are the forcibly displaced populations and their host communities?	• Where do the forcibly displaced people live? • What water risks do they face?

Source: World Bank.

The first question is addressed in chapter 2, and chapter 3 addresses the second and third questions. The concluding chapter 4 discusses interventions to respond to the water risks faced by the forcibly displaced populations and their host communities and to build resilience in the long term, to prevent water-related challenges from undermining livelihoods and economies.

NOTE

1. Gulf countries include Bahrain, Iraq, Islamic Republic of Iran, Kuwait, Oman, Qatar, Saudi Arabia, and the United Arab Emirates.

REFERENCES

Borgomeo, E., N. Al-Mudaffar Fawzi, J. W. Hall, A. Jägerskog, A. Nicol, C. W. Sadoff, M. Salman, N. Santos, and M. Talhami. 2020. "Tackling the Trickle: Ensuring Sustainable Water Management in the Arab Region." *Earth's Future* 8 (5): e2020EF001495.

Devarajan, S., and E. Ianchovichina. 2018. "A Broken Social Contract, Not High Inequality, Led to the Arab Spring." *Review of Income and Wealth* 64: S5–S25.

Elitok, S. P., and C. Fröhlich. 2019. "Displacement, Refugees, and Forced Migration in the MENA Region." In *Routledge International Handbook of Migration Studies*, edited by Steven J. Gold and Stephanie J. Nawyn. Abingdon, Oxon, UK: Routledge.

GMDAC (Global Migration Data Analysis Centre). 2021. "Migration Data in Northern Africa." Berlin: International Organization for Migration. https://migrationdataportal.org/regional-data-overview/northern-africa.

IDMC (Internal Displacement Monitoring Centre). 2020. *Internal Displacement 2020: Mid-year Update.* https://www.internal-displacement.org/sites/default/files/publications/documents/2020%20Mid-year%20update.pdf.

IDMC (Internal Displacement Monitoring Centre) and NRC (Norwegian Refugee Council). 2020. *Global Report on Internal Displacement*. Geneva: IDMC. https://www.internal-displacement.org/sites/default/files/publications /documents/2019-IDMC-GRID.pdf.

McDowall, D. 1996. *A Modern History of the Kurds*. London: IB Tauris.

Swain, A., and A. Jägerskog. 2016. *Emerging Security Threats in the Middle East: The Impact of Climate Change and Globalization*. London: Rowman & Littlefield.

UN DESA (United Nations Department of Economic and Social Affairs). 2019. "International Migrant Stock 2019." https://www.un.org/en/development /desa/population/migration/data/estimates2/estimates19.asp.

UNHCR (United Nations High Commissioner for Refugees). 2018. *Fourth Regional Survey on Syrian Refugees' Perceptions and Intentions on Return to Syria (RPIS)*. Geneva: UNHCR.

UNHCR (United Nations High Commissioner for Refugees). 2020. *Global Trends: Forced Displacement in 2019*. Geneva: UNHCR. https://www.unhcr .org/5ee200e37.pdf.

Verner, D., ed. 2012. *Adaptation to a Changing Climate in the Arab Countries: A Case for Adaptation Governance and Leadership in Building Climate Resilience*. Washington, DC: World Bank.

World Bank. 2017a. *Beyond Scarcity: Water Security in the Middle East and North Africa*. Middle East and North Africa Development Report. Washington, DC: World Bank.

World Bank. 2017b. *Forcibly Displaced: Toward a Development Approach Supporting Refugees, the Internally Displaced, and Their Hosts*. Washington, DC: World Bank.

World Bank. 2017c. *The Toll of War: The Economic and Social Consequences of the Conflict in Syria*. Washington, DC: World Bank.

World Bank. 2020. *The Fallout of War: The Regional Consequences of the Conflict in Syria*. Washington, DC: World Bank.

Wrathall, D. J., J. Hoek, A. Walters, and A. Devenish. 2018. "Water Stress and Human Migration: A Global, Georeferenced Review of Empirical Research." Land and Water Discussion Paper, Food and Agriculture Organization of the United Nations, Rome.

Zaveri, Esha, Jason Russ, Amjad Khan, Richard Damania, Edoardo Borgomeo, and Anders Jägerskog. 2021. *Ebb and Flow: Volume 1. Water, Migration, and Development*. Washington, DC: World Bank.

CHAPTER TWO

WHY AND IN WHAT CONTEXTS DOES WATER CONTRIBUTE TO CONFLICT AND FORCED DISPLACEMENT?

We left because of the conflict. Our house was wrecked by a bomb and the village became isolated as everyone left. Thus, we left.

—Name withheld, Syrian refugee, Zaatari camp, Jordan, September 2020

Regional conflict is rooted in the political side of issues, with many levels of political conflict that took the region into the chaos it experiences today.

—Name withheld, Jordanian geopolitical expert, July 2020

KEY HIGHLIGHTS

- Contrary to common belief, the evidence linking water risks with conflict and forced displacement in the Middle East and North Africa is not unequivocal.

- Case studies and event data suggest that water risks are more frequently related to cooperation than to conflict, at both the domestic and international levels.

- Although conflict is an uncertain consequence of water risks, the contrary is a real and concerning outcome of conflict: since 2011, there have been at least 180 instances of targeting of water infrastructure in the region's conflicts in Gaza, Libya, Syrian Arab Republic, and the Republic of Yemen.

- Climate change and soaring demand are adding pressures on economies and livelihood systems that are dependent on already depleted and degraded water resources: this changing nature of water, paired with the changing nature of conflict, suggests that the future nexus of water, forced displacement, and conflict might look very different from the past.

INTRODUCTION

This chapter addresses the most debated aspect of the water and human mobility story in the Middle East and North Africa—the supposed influence of water risks on forced displacement and conflict, especially in the context of the Syrian civil war. To provide a policy-relevant synthesis, the existing evidence is grouped under a set of three questions and complemented with specific case studies and statistical analysis of historical event databases. Novel insights from qualitative surveys are also presented to provide additional perspectives on the topic. First, the chapter examines the evidence on the links between water risks and forced displacement in the region. Second, it reviews the evidence linking water and conflict, paying particular attention to the role of forced displacement as an intervening variable linking water and conflict. Third, it asks if water might be a source of tension and conflict between forcibly displaced populations and the host communities. The chapter concludes with a forward look to consider how water scarcity and variability under climate change, combined with the changing nature of conflict, might affect these dynamics.

WHAT IS THE EVIDENCE ON THE LINKS BETWEEN WATER RISKS AND FORCED DISPLACEMENT?

Although it is difficult to disaggregate drivers of human mobility and their relative importance, water risks emerge as important factors influencing decisions to move in specific contexts. Survey data from Iraq and Libya suggest that small-scale forced displacement takes place in response to water scarcity and lack of access to water services. In Iraq, multiple surveys of internally displaced persons (IDPs) from different years identify water scarcity as one of the key drivers of forced displacement and reasons for returning (or not) to places of origin (IOM 2012, 2019; Guiu 2020). In these surveys, water scarcity refers to both lack of water to support agriculture and livestock and lack of drinking water services. In some governorates, especially in southern Iraq, more than 25 percent of IDPs cited water scarcity as the main reason for displacement and also the main reason preventing them from returning to their place of origin (2010 survey). In a follow-up survey in 2019, the International Organization for Migration in Iraq identified 21,314 IDPs from the southern and central governorates who were displaced due to drinking water issues caused by high salinity content or waterborne diseases (IOM and Deltares 2020). Most of these individuals came from the four governorates in the south (Missan, Muthanna, Thi-Qar, and Basra), where 5,347 families were displaced because of water quantity and quality issues (IOM 2019). Given southern Iraq's ongoing water issues, characterized by a convergence of dilapidated infrastructure, governance gaps, and high vulnerability to climate change (including seawater intrusion), migration emerges as a key option for rural families to adapt to increasing water scarcity and declining water quality. Beyond water scarcity, access to basic water services can also act as a factor in influencing decisions to move in specific contexts, as suggested by surveys of IDPs in Libya. Although water services are not mentioned as a primary "push" factor for leaving the place of origin, the availability of basic services—safe drinking water, sanitation facilities, housing, energy, education, and health care—emerges as a primary "pull factor" among IDPs. As shown in figure 2.1, access to basic services, including water, is among a set of reasons cited by IDPs for coming to their current locations in Libya.

Although evidence of local instances of displacement in response to water risks exists, there is limited evidence of water risks causing large-scale forced displacement. As noted in *Ebb and Flow: Volume 1*, the water and human mobility story is a story of nuance (Zaveri et al. 2021). The impact of water risks on decisions to move depends on context, on the characteristics of these water risks, and on their interactions with other social and economic drivers that influence the nature and scale of human mobility. Adaptation responses, from the household to the national level, also play a key role in influencing this relationship. Across the Middle East and North Africa, existing evidence suggests that socioeconomic and security factors are the key drivers influencing large-scale population displacement (World Bank

FIGURE 2.1: Reasons for Leaving Place of Origin and Coming to Current Location among IDP Communities in Libya, June 2020

a. Reasons for leaving place of origin

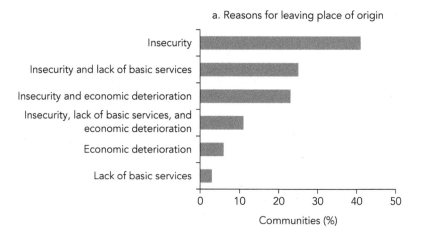

b. Reasons for coming to current location

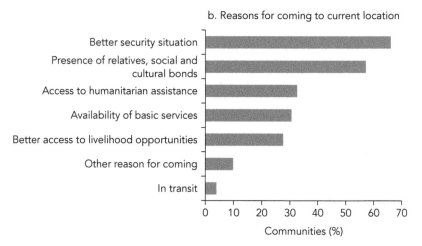

Source: IOM 2020.
Note: Respondents could select more than one reason. Basic services include safe drinking water, sanitation facilities, housing, energy, education, and health care. Figure shows the reasons for choosing the current location identified by key informants and reported at the community (*muhalla*) level for 483 communities hosting IDPs.

2017b; IOM 2017). World Bank surveys and economic analysis based on data from Algeria, the Arab Republic of Egypt, Morocco, Syria, and the Republic of Yemen show that water-related factors are not a primary driver of human mobility in the region (Wodon et al. 2014). Other factors related to job prospects in cities, security, and the socioeconomic situation of the household are more important drivers. Experts interviewed for this report also identified a small influence of water risks on human mobility and conflict relative to socioeconomic and political factors (box 2.1).

The context-specific nature of the water and human mobility relationship invites caution and holds a few key insights. First, the relationship between water and forced displacement, especially large-

BOX 2.1: Influence of Water Risks on Migration and Conflict Relative to Socioeconomic and Political Factors

To elicit subject matter expertise on the relationship between water, conflict, and migration in the Middle East and North Africa (MENA), nine experts were interviewed. The group of nine experts comprised a sample of researchers, practitioners, and policy makers working on water, conflict, and migration issues in MENA. Their areas of expertise represented a range of disciplines (engineering, economics, political science), organizations (universities, nongovernmental organizations, donors, government), and geographies within MENA. The interview and data analysis protocols were developed by the World Bank in collaboration with the West Asia-North Africa (WANA) Institute and then administered by the WANA Institute, modeled after the expert elicitation approach presented in Mach et al. (2019) and described in more detail in appendix C. Expert elicitation is a well-known and tested method for documenting expert judgment about available evidence and supporting public policy decision making (Morgan 2014). Expert elicitation has already been used to study the global relationship between climate and conflict, with findings suggesting that socioeconomic development and state capacity are substantially more influential than climate in driving international armed conflict (Mach et al. 2019).

During the interviews, each expert ranked factors that most influence migration and conflict, drawing from a list of 15 and 12 factors, respectively. Each expert also ranked the same factors on the basis of how much uncertainty there was about their influence on migration and conflict. Following the guidance of the International Organization for Migration, "migration" is here understood in a broad sense as an umbrella term, not defined under international law, reflecting the common lay understanding of a person who moves away from his or her place of usual residence, whether within a country or across an international border, temporarily or permanently, and for a variety of reasons.

The subject matter experts agreed that water factors, such as crop failure and drought, had affected migration in the region. However, they also ranked other factors, such as war, unemployment, and corruption, as much more influential drivers of migration compared with water-related issues (figure B2.1.1). When asked to rank these factors in terms of the most uncertainty about their influence on migration, the experts identified "high temperatures" and "high risks from natural hazards" as having the most uncertain influence on migration.

box continues next page

BOX 2.1: Experts Identify Small Influence of Water Risks on Migration and Conflict Relative to Socioeconomic and Political Factors *continued*

FIGURE B2.1.1: Factors that Influence Migration in the Middle East and North Africa, by Influence and Uncertainty

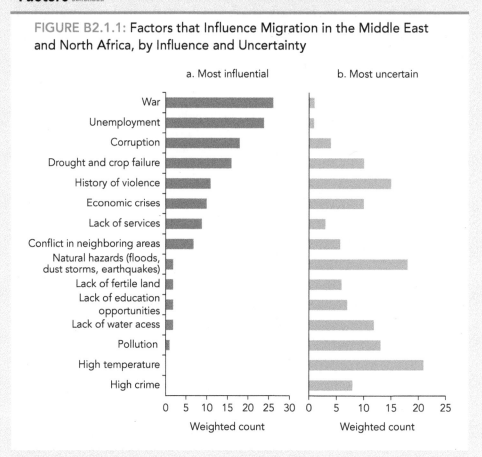

Note: Each expert ranked five factors in terms of influence in driving migration (panel a) and uncertainty about their influence (panel b). The rankings for each factor across experts were summed and are shown in the figure.

When evaluating conflict drivers and their uncertainty, experts agreed that mistrust of government, external intervention, unemployment, and corruption are all influential drivers. Across the experts, climate-related water risks (droughts) were deemed to have little or no influence on conflict risk. The experts also indicated that there was more uncertainty about the influence on conflict of water risks, unemployment, illiberal democracy, and natural resource dependency (figure B2.1.2).

box continues next page

BOX 2.1: Experts Identify Small Influence of Water Risks on Migration and Conflict Relative to Socioeconomic and Political Factors *continued*

FIGURE B2.1.2: Ranking of Factors That Most Influence Armed Conflict in the Middle East and North Africa

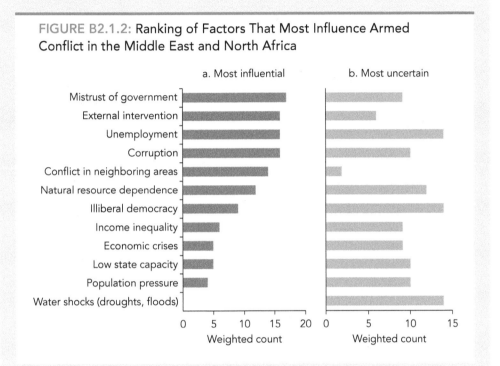

Note: Each expert ranked five factors in terms of influence in driving conflict (panel a) and uncertainty about their influence (panel b). The rankings for each factor across experts were summed and are shown in the figure. One respondent opted out of answering this question; hence results responses from eight experts.

Finally, the experts agreed that the influence of water risks on migration was set to increase in the future as the impacts of climate change materialized. When asked if water risks led to changes in migration rates, experts agreed that water risks led to moderate changes in migration rates at present, but that they expected substantial changes to occur under climate change (figure B2.1.3). Although these findings might not be surprising, the approach shows that agreement and common ground on complex and multidisciplinary policy questions can emerge and that expert elicitation offers one way of approaching this complexity.

box continues next page

BOX 2.1: Experts Identify Small Influence of Water Risks on Migration and Conflict Relative to Socioeconomic and Political Factors *continued*

FIGURE B2.1.3: Changes in the Influence of Water Risks on Migration Rates under Increasing Climate Change

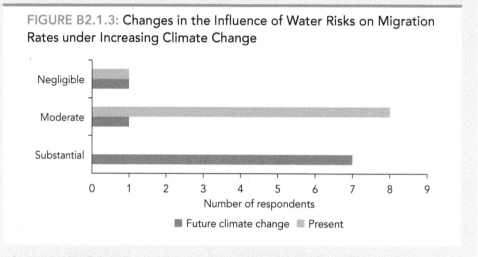

Source: World Bank, based on expert elicitations conducted by the WANA Institute.
Note: For two scenarios, the figure shows the number of respondents suggesting that climate change leads to negligible, moderate, or substantial changes in migration rates compared with present conditions.

scale forced displacement, is complex. While water risks can affect forced displacement, the complexity of interacting factors influencing individual and household choices to move means that it is not possible or particularly helpful for policy to identify water migrants in the Middle East and North Africa. Second, there are local instances of forced displacement in response to water-related issues (notably lack of basic water services and drought), but this displacement is mostly internal and not transborder. Third, research and policy should focus on the effects that water and agricultural policy might have in exacerbating or mitigating the effects of water risks on vulnerable populations, their livelihoods, and income-generating activities. This is particularly important given the major water governance challenges in the Middle East and North Africa, combined with challenging biophysical conditions (World Bank 2017a). While the complexity of human mobility decisions is well known, there is still a tendency to simplify the issue, even identifying population movement as a crucial link or intervening variable between environmental stresses and conflict, as discussed in the next section.

WHAT IS THE EVIDENCE ON THE LINKS BETWEEN WATER AND CONFLICT?

It is often assumed that water risks, notably drought, contribute to forced displacement and conflict. However, as this section explains, the context-specific nature of the water and displacement relationship invites caution. The section begins by considering the often-cited example of Syria as an entry point into the broader literature on the links between water risks and conflict.

Although International Headlines Identified Drought as Implicated in Syria's War, These Claims Have Been Questioned

Although media reports have suggested that drought-induced displacement is at the root of the Syrian conflict, these claims have been questioned and disproven. According to this narrative, the long Syrian drought that started in 2007 contributed to agricultural failures in the northeast. In turn, this led to forced mass displacement from the rural areas to the large urban centers in the south, where internal migrants contributed to the uprisings in 2011 that marked the onset of the war (Gleick 2014; Kelley et al. 2015). In this view, forced displacement then emerges as a key intervening variable between drought and conflict. The 2007–10 drought undoubtedly contributed to reducing agricultural incomes and devastating livelihoods, with empirical evidence suggesting that at least some level of human displacement took place following the drought from the most affected areas in the northeast (Ash and Obradovich 2020). However, the scale of human displacement following the drought is not known, and no consistent estimates are available (Fröhlich 2016; Selby et al. 2017). Interview data further suggest that protests in urban areas in the south—where unrest first started—were led by young and educated people, not by rural migrants from drought-stricken northeastern Syria (Fröhlich 2016), and that the issues at the core of the protests were unrelated to drought and agriculture; instead, they were related to security concerns, corruption, and human rights issues (Daoudy 2020).

Though the links between the Syrian conflict and drought have been contested, this does not mean that the 2007 drought did not have catastrophic impacts on agricultural production and livelihoods, or that Syria's climate is not changing (box 2.2). National wheat harvests declined to 2.1 million tons compared with 4.7 million tons achieved in previous years.[1] This level of impact seems at odds with the high level of water resource development that took place in Syria in the preceding decades, including a doubling of the area under irrigation from 0.6 million hectares in 1985 to 1.35 million hectares in 2010, much of it dedicated to wheat (Ward and

BOX 2.2: Climate Change in the Syrian Arab Republic

Many climate change impacts are already occurring in the Syrian Arab Republic. Precipitation has dropped significantly in some sites. Winter rainfall totals have declined significantly at some sites in northern and western Syria. Some changes are comparable to the large interannual variability associated with shifts in the storm track across the eastern Mediterranean—for example, since the 1950s, annual rainfall in Aleppo has declined by about 90 millimeters (a 30 percent decrease). Looking forward, rainfall is expected to become more variable, with some climate models also showing decreasing precipitation totals by 2050.

Climate change is also expected to alter the timing and availability of water resources. Syria's future water security will depend, in part, on changes in snowpack and residual flows from the Euphrates, which could decline by 11 percent with a 7 percent reduction in rainfall, and by 60 percent with a 5°C warming (there is already more than 2 degrees of warming). An increase in temperature combined with reduced precipitation could lead to a reduction in runoff and groundwater recharge and, therefore, a reduction in the water resources available for human, agricultural, and industrial use. Even without these projected impacts, Syria already faces a water crisis. Estimates show that available resources amount to 16 billion cubic meters per year, and total use has reached 19.1 billion cubic meters per year (before the war). In consequence, the water balance of Syria is negative, with a deficit of 3.1 billion cubic meters per year, with significant variation across basins. Only three basins have a positive balance, and the remaining have considerable negative balances. The groundwater situation is particularly dire: water tables have decreased enormously in many areas—up to 57 meters in the Orontes and Khabour basins during the 1990s.

Sources: Verner 2011; Breisinger et al. 2013.

Ruckstuhl 2017). Government policy facilitated cultivation ever deeper into the *badiya* (desert), promoting unregulated groundwater use through energy subsidies and the subsidized expansion of irrigated systems (Barnes 2009; de Châtel 2014). These water policies failed to balance short-term productivity growth through groundwater expansion with the long-term negative impacts of groundwater depletion (Aw-Hassan et al. 2014) and the discriminatory systems of land tenure rights along ethnic lines. Some groups were favored over others, creating resentment toward the government among the groups and communities being discriminated against (Daoudy 2020). Much of this irrigation adopted water-inefficient methods and drove groundwater depletion, thus inevitably confirming the paradox of supply: the expansion of irrigation in dry areas without careful planning and regulation of water use promotes the cultivation of water-intensive crops and wasteful consumption (Damania et al. 2017). During a drought, irrigation cannot meet these increasing crop water requirements, leading to large-scale crop failure. Poor irrigation planning can paradoxically amplify the impacts of droughts and increase vulnerability to climate change, including movement of people, as shown in volume 1 of *Ebb and Flow* (Zaveri et al. 2021). When combined with the government's shift in 2005 to a social market economy, and the subsequent abrupt removal of agricultural subsidies and increased attention to urban areas, these short-sighted water and agricultural policies greatly exacerbated vulnerability to drought and created additional hardships for rural Syrians (Daoudy 2020). Although the 2007–10 drought also affected neighboring Jordan, it did not lead to any large-scale impacts on agricultural production and livelihoods, partially because of the greater attention paid to drought policy in that country and its efforts to reduce dependency on agriculture given water-scarcity constraints (Feitelson and Tubi 2017).

At the Subnational Level, Water Issues Are More Often Related to Cooperation Than to Conflict

Case studies and analyses of event databases suggest that water issues at the subnational level rarely lead to cooperative or conflictive events, and that when they do so, they are more often related to cooperation than conflict. In other words: (a) most water-related events are neither cooperative nor conflictive; and (b) more often than not, individuals and communities within countries tend to cooperate when faced with water risks, in particular water shortages. This insight emerges from an analysis of Water-Related Intrastate Conflict and Cooperation (WARICC), the world's largest event data set on domestic water-related conflicts and cooperation. WARICC contains a record of water events that occurred in the Middle East and North Africa region from 1997 to 2009 (Bernauer et al. 2012). In this database, an event can involve unilateral actions by individuals, firms, nongovernmental organizations, or state authorities, or interactions between them (Bernauer et al. 2012), such as construction of a water supply plant or water supply cuts to a neighborhood. Each event is assigned a value from +5 (most cooperative) to –5 (most conflictive). An event is considered cooperative when these actions or interactions over water-related issues likely or actually improve the water quality or quantity at the domestic level (for example, national government inaugurates a water project, or a ministerial meeting agrees to expand access to water in the country). On the other hand, a conflictive event takes place when this action or interaction over water-related issues actually worsens water quantity or quality (for example, rebel militias take control of water wells, or protests over water shortages turn deadly). The data set involves issue coding; this means that events are classified as either cooperative or conflictive on the basis of the coder's interpretation of an improvement or deterioration of water security and not a specific counterfactual event. Although this approach has some limitations, it offers complementary insights to quantitative assessments of water-related variables and conflict, and it also allows for the study of cooperative events, which are typically ignored in most quantitative models (box 2.3).

BOX 2.3: Complementary Approaches to Study the Links between Water-Related Variables, Migration, and Conflict

The understanding of the links between water and conflict relies on complementary approaches. A first approach builds on empirical models that draw inferences on the basis of the effects of water-related variables (typically rainfall) on conflict risk or intensity (defined in different ways, including number of battle-related deaths but also low-intensity conflict such as riots). These approaches typically exploit variations in rainfall over time that are plausibly independent of other variables that might affect conflict risk (Hsiang, Burke, and Miguel 2013). Although these approaches have yielded significant insights into the links between climate and conflict, they have also been criticized for selecting cases in which only conflict is present (Adams et al. 2018) and for lacking sufficient understanding of the social, economic, and political factors at play (Buhaug 2010). More generally, these approaches typically overlook cooperative events, focusing only on the conflict dimension. This means that although climate–conflict research has analyzed links between water-related variables (mostly meteorological drought and rainfall shocks) and conflict, it has overlooked cooperative outcomes (Koubi 2019).

A second approach uses coding of historical events related to water. This approach requires coding textual information, such as newspaper articles or press releases describing a specific water-related event, into numerical values. Although this approach allows coders to focus on specific event types of interest, it also requires them to interpret information and assign it to a limited set of categories (Ruggeri, Gizelis, and Dorussen 2011; Bernauer et al. 2012). The focus on specific event types means that this approach considers both conflictive and cooperative events and that it examines events that directly involve water or water-related variables, for example, transboundary river basins. In doing so, this approach sheds light on the frequency, intensity, and type of conflictive and cooperative events related to water. Compared with the first approach, this approach does not attempt to build a good quantitative model of water-related variables and conflict. Rather, it is the data coders who

box continues next page

BOX 2.3: **Complementary Approaches to Study the Links between Water-Related Variables, Migration, and Conflict** *continued*

identify the causal link between water and conflict or cooperation on the basis of their interpretation of the information source. As described in appendix B, this also comes with its own limitations because data quality and coder biases can affect the results.

Given the complex dynamics between global environmental change and human societies, it is important to pursue a plurality of approaches (Solow 2013; Mach and Kraan 2021). *Ebb and Flow: Volume 1* (Zaveri et al. 2021), is largely based on the first approach, while chapter 2 of *Ebb and Flow: Volume 2* builds on well-known event databases of domestic and international water events to build a picture of both cooperation and conflict in relation to water in the region (Wolf 1999; Wolf, Yoffe, and Giordano 2003; Bernauer et al. 2012; Böhmelt et al. 2014). The choice to adopt both approaches stems from the recognition that unless a plurality of methods is adopted, it will be difficult to shed light on the complex links between water, human mobility, and conflict.

The analysis of the database shows that while cooperation dominates water-related interactions occurring domestically, there is considerable variation among countries and subregions, and most water-related events were neither conflictive nor cooperative. Over the time period covered in the database (1997–2009), about half of all water-related events did not have any positive or negative impact on water quantity or quality (figure 2.2). About 28 percent of the events were cooperative, and 21 percent conflictive. This finding is confirmed when additional database specifications are considered (see appendix B) and when key water-related constraints, such as challenging access to groundwater, are taken into account. In the Middle East and North Africa, water-scarce areas are more likely to experience instances of water cooperation, including in areas with difficult-to-access groundwater (Döring 2020). This confirms evidence from other parts of the world suggesting that long-term exposure to water scarcity strengthens water users' preference for cooperation (Haseeb 2020; Nie, Yang, and Tu 2020).

Although the prevalence of cooperative events is encouraging, this should not lead to downplaying the incidence of conflictive events. As shown in figure 2.2, conflictive events prevail when values in the interval greater than 4 or lower than –4 are considered (that is, the "tails" of the distribution). Hence, although water overall leads to more cooperation than conflict, there is also plenty of evidence showing how it leads to physical violence and deterioration of security conditions within countries.

FIGURE 2.2: Number of Domestic Events Related to Water Quality/Quantity in the Middle East and North Africa Displayed on a Conflict/Cooperation Scale, 1997–2009

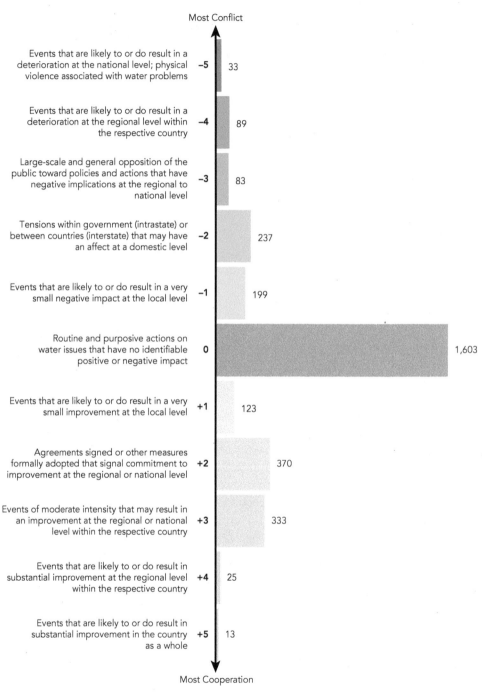

Source: World Bank using data from Bernauer et al. 2012.

When It Comes to International Relations, Historical Records Suggest That Water Engenders Cooperation More Than Conflict Does

Event data coding is the most widely used approach to understand whether international freshwater resources elicit conflict or cooperation (Bernauer and Böhmelt 2020). The International Water Event database captures events related to international river basins between 1948 and 2008, assigning them a value between –7 (maximum conflict, or war) and +7 (maximum cooperation) (Wolf 1998, 2007; De Stefano et al. 2010). Examples of conflictive events include strong verbal expression of hostility against another country regarding water or military action, while examples of cooperative events are a water pipeline connecting two countries to deliver water, or scientific agreements to set up cooperative working groups over water. Although this data set ends in 2008 and does not include events relating to aquifers, it still provides helpful information on the historical occurrence of conflict and cooperation related to international waters in the region.

The distribution of cooperation and conflict events across all international river basins in the Middle East and North Africa from 1948 to 2008 is shown in figure 2.3. As observed for domestic water events, cooperation is the most frequent type of interaction over international river basins. Out of the 975 events recorded in the database for the region, 56 percent were cooperative, 37 percent were conflictive, and 8 percent were neutral. This greater frequency of cooperative events is confirmed even when certain specific regional conflicts and countries are removed from the database as a way of testing the robustness of this result (see appendix B). Even if the more recent period is considered (post 2000), cooperative events are still more prevalent. Given the number of armed conflicts that have plagued the Middle East and North Africa region over the past five decades, the observation that historically water issues have brought countries to cooperate is notable.

Although it is encouraging to find that cooperation is more frequent than conflict overall, this should not induce complacency because more than 37 percent of the events are indeed conflictive, with conflict prevailing in the tails of the distribution. When the most negative or positive, or conflictive or cooperative, events (less than –5, greater than +5) in figure 2.3 are considered, then conflictive events appear to be more frequent. This suggests that the highest forms of transboundary water cooperation, such as treaties and agreements over shared water resources (event types 5 and 6), have been typically harder to achieve than technical and economic agreements (event types 3 and 4). At the other side of the event distribution, although formal declarations of war have not been registered, extensive war acts related to water have been reported, especially in relation to the Israeli-Palestinian conflict. Table 2.1 presents examples of international water events in the Middle East and North Africa between 1948 and 2008, ranked on a conflict/cooperation scale.

FIGURE 2.3: Number of International Water Events in the Middle East and North Africa Displayed on a Conflict/Cooperation Scale, 1948–2008

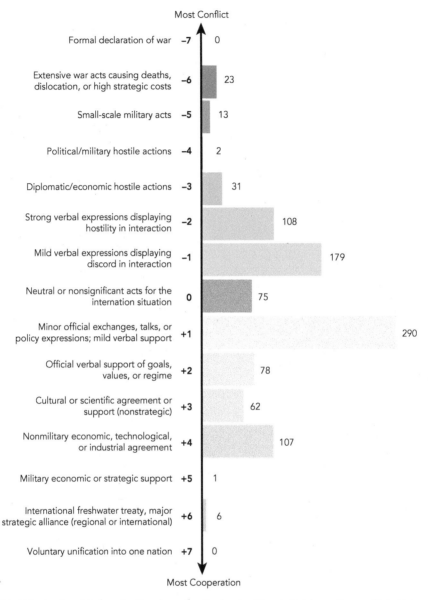

Source: World Bank using data from the Transboundary Freshwater Dispute Database, Oregon State University.

While cooperation is dominating the interactions, the quantitative results in figure 2.3 based on event coding may not provide a full picture. In recognition of this, the *quality* of the cooperation has increasingly received attention. This perspective underscores the importance of understanding power asymmetries between countries and their effect on the possibility of achieving equitable outcomes, which is key to building durable peace (Zeitoun and Warner 2006). Furthermore, the relation between two or

Table 2.1: Examples of International Water Events in the Middle East and North Africa, Ranked on a Conflict/Cooperation Scale, 1948–2008

Conflict/ cooperation scale	Date	Countries involved	Event summary
−6	August 8, 1969	Egypt, Arab Rep., and Israel	Israel attacks Port Said and freshwater canal in Egypt, Arab Rep.
−5	March 27, 1958	Israel and Syrian Arab Republic	Syrian Arab Republic clashes with Israel for third day near Lake Huleh project.
−4	May 1, 1975	Iraq and Syrian Arab Republic	In May 1975, Syrian Arab Republic closed its airspace to Iraqi flights and both Syrian Arab Republic and Iraq reportedly transferred troops to their mutual border. Mediation on the part of Saudi Arabia broke the increasing tension, and on June 3, the parties arrived at an agreement that averted the impending violence. Although the terms of the agreement were not made public, Iraqi sources are cited as privately stating that the agreement called for Syrian Arab Republic to keep 40 percent of the flow of the Euphrates within its borders, and to allow the remaining 60 percent through to Iraq.
−3	March 15, 1999	Israel and Jordan	A Jordanian official states that the government "strongly" rejects the request of Meir Ben-Meir, Israel's water commissioner, to reduce the flow of water to Jordan. Although the peace treaty does not address reductions due to droughts, the water commissioner requested that Jordan accept a reduction of approximately 60 percent in its 1999 water allocation because the Jordan River had only received approximately 40 percent of its normal annual streamflow.
−2	June 6, 1975	Iraq and Syrian Arab Republic	Iraq claims that the lack of Euphrates water because of Syrian Arab Republic withdrawals has destroyed 70 percent of crops.
−1	February 28, 1991	Iraq, Syrian Arab Republic, and Turkey	The leader of the True Path party in Turkey states that Turkey does not owe water to anyone, just as Turkey does not claim anyone else's water.
0	February 6, 1960	Iraq, Israel, and United Nations	Iraq informs the United Nations of its opposition to Israel's water diversion plan.
1	April 12, 1967	Iraq and Syrian Arab Republic	Iraq and Syrian Arab Republic confer on the distribution of water from the River Euphrates.
3	July 13, 1964	Algeria and Tunisia	Algeria and Tunisia agree to undertake a joint study on construction of a dam on the Medjerda River.
4	January 1, 1996	Israel and Jordan	Israel delivers water (as per the peace treaty allocation) to Jordan via the Beit Zera pipeline. The agreement stipulates that 10 million cubic meters be transferred during the winter of 1996 and 20 million cubic meters in the summer of 1996.
6	October 26, 1994	Israel and Jordan	Israel and Jordan sign the Treaty of Peace between the state of Israel and the Hashemite Kingdom of Jordan. The peace treaty includes settlement of water and land rights disputes; agreement on full diplomatic relations within one month; and commitment to joint projects in tourism, water, energy, transport, environmental protection, and drug control.

Source: Transboundary Freshwater Dispute Database, Oregon State University.

more countries over a water resource often includes both cooperative and conflictive events happening more or less at the same time. In other words, there could be instances of verbal hostility between countries over water and at the same time scientific working groups or formal committees could still be meeting to coordinate and cooperate over the shared water resource.

Policy Failures Exacerbate Water Risks and Fragility

Although historical records suggest that water is more often a driver of cooperation than of conflict, this should not induce complacency. Global reviews and in-depth case studies provide detailed descriptions of instances in which policy failures to sustainably and equitably manage and allocate scarce water resources contribute to social tensions and severely undermine livelihoods (Sadoff, Borgomeo, and de Waal 2017). This is also confirmed by in-depth case studies for the Middle East and North Africa, which suggest that preexisting socioeconomic grievances in combination with a drought or water shortage can drive domestic water tensions, especially in the absence of strong institutions (Ide et al. 2020). The 2018 water crisis in Basra is a stark reminder of the tensions that can arise following water shortages and declines of service quality in a context of protracted armed conflict, sanctions, and grievances (box 2.4).

Water risks can act as intermediate variables rather than direct drivers of conflict, in contexts characterized by socioeconomic fragility and political grievances (Feitelson and Tubi 2017). For example, prior to 2011, access to land and water resources was highly politicized in Syria, with some groups favored over others. Failure to manage the social and environmental consequences of the Syrian government's push to expand irrigation in the 1980s through the 1990s exacerbated the vulnerabilities of the rural poor and their economic disenfranchisement (Barnes 2009). As discussed earlier in this chapter, promotion of water-intensive agriculture in dry areas made agricultural livelihoods more vulnerable to drought in the long run. In addition, certain groups, notably Syrian Kurds, were denied access to agricultural land, further worsening domestic inequality and access to opportunity, factors that contributed to further fragility and polarization in society (Daoudy 2020). This failure to manage the social dimensions of water contributed to a vicious cycle whereby water-related issues heightened grievances, contributing to further destabilization of already fragile contexts (Sadoff, Borgomeo, and de Waal 2017).

Provision of water services is another way through which water is related to conflict in the Middle East and North Africa. Provision of basic services has long been recognized as a strategy adopted by nonstate actors during or following an armed conflict to build legitimacy and extract resources from populations (Grynkewich 2008; Cammett and MacLean 2014). These actors exploit their armed capacity to first gain control of basic services and then wield this power to further erode state legitimacy. In the

BOX 2.4: Basra: A Hot Spot of Water Scarcity and Fragility

Iraq's Basra governorate faces a water crisis. For decades, the governorate's population of more than 4 million people has struggled to receive safe access to drinking water. Once known as the "Venice of the East," Basra now faces an existential water crisis that is already undermining livelihoods and stability. Since the 1980s, high levels of pollutants, increased salinity, and upstream water resource development, paired with weak local water governance, have resulted in the progressive degradation of freshwater supplies in the Basra governorate. Over the past decade, there has been an acceleration of the water crisis, with freshwater scarcity in the governorate leading to an increase in conflict in agricultural areas as well as increased migration from and within the city of Basra. The failure to preserve water resources in the south is not only driving displacement to cities but also is reinforcing local perceptions of marginalization and exclusion (Al-Mudaffar Fawzi et al. 2016). By 2018, about 87 percent of Basra's agricultural land had been lost and most of the governorate's water buffalo and cattle had died, compared with data from the 1970s (Human Rights Watch 2019). In turn, this has led many people to move to urban centers, where services are already strained by decades of conflict, sanctions, and governance challenges, or to encroach on private lands in search of water and feed for livestock (Norwegian Refugee Council 2018). In communities receiving forcibly displaced persons, access to drinking water and pasture rights for livestock can be a source of tension. As rural populations are displaced due to water scarcity, water buffalos are often shot by host community members for grazing in areas farmed by residents (Norwegian Refugee Council 2018).

Lack of water access has also heightened the risk of a public health crisis in Basra. In the summer of 2018, about 118,000 Basrans were hospitalized because of water-related illnesses (Human Rights Watch 2019). During the water crisis, hundreds of Basrans protested against the lack of government response and the poor health and water services provided (Human Rights Watch 2019). The crisis sparked more violent protests, as residents took to the streets to challenge the government response to water shortages, lack of electricity, and unemployment. The 2018 crisis is a reflection of the cumulative impacts of protracted armed conflict, sanctions, and mismanagement of water supplies, and their rippling effects on livelihoods and political stability in fragile contexts.

long run, provision of basic services by nonstate actors can politically benefit these actors and affect peace and state-building processes.

Although water policy failures can compound fragility, water policy can also be used to prevent conflict and help build peace. In post-conflict settings, access to water and to functioning and well-managed ecosystems—providing livelihood opportunities—represents an important tenet of peacebuilding. Weinthal, Troell, and Nakayama (2014) define peacebuilding objectives as (a) establishing security, (b) restoring basic services, (c) revitalizing the economy and enhancing livelihoods, and (d) rebuilding governance and inclusive political processes. The provision of water in both conflict and post-conflict societies represents a key tenet for allowing this rebuilding to occur; it also contributes to installing legitimacy and it is an important part of the social contract. Equitable and efficient water resource management and delivery can assist in meeting these objectives and as such also has a transboundary dimension. The 1994 peace agreement between Israel and Jordan is an example of this. The agreement makes provision for storing water flows from the Yarmouk River (tributary to the Jordan River) during the wintertime in Lake Tiberias in Israel (when water flow is, in relative terms, more plentiful) for release during the summer months when Jordan has higher needs. This arrangement has functioned without major challenges for well over two decades. It shows how cooperation on water can serve to promote the provision of basic services and strengthen security, thereby supporting peacebuilding (Jägerskog 2018).

Water Is Increasingly a Casualty and Weapon of Conflict

Whereas conflict is an uncertain consequence of water crises, the converse—that water risks are very often directly related to conflict—is real and has been observed in parts of the Middle East and North Africa. Conflict has caused significant damage to water infrastructure and services (Gleick 2019). Heavy fighting with explosive weaponry means that the region's water and sanitation infrastructure, alongside the electricity infrastructure on which it largely depends, has suffered regular and serious damage (ICRC 2015).

Water is often a victim of conflict in the region, with instances of water infrastructure targeting increasing in the past decade. In Syria, a World Bank damage assessment suggested that 457 water supply and sanitation assets had been damaged, meaning that about two-thirds of the country's water treatment plants and half of its pumping stations were destroyed (World Bank 2017c). And the damage is not only collateral. Since 2011, water infrastructure has been directly targeted by warring parties to inflict damage on opposing sides. A database compiled on the basis of reports by humanitarian organizations, United Nations agencies, think tanks, human rights groups, and media reports suggests that from 2011 to 2018 there have been more than 100 instances of water infrastructure targeting in the region's conflicts in Gaza, Libya, Syria, and the Republic of Yemen (figure 2.4) (Sowers, Weinthal, and Zawahri 2017). In Libya, there has been an increase in attacks on water infrastructure, which led to water supplies being cut to approximately 2 million people in Tripoli in 2020

FIGURE 2.4: Instances of Water Infrastructure Targeting in the Middle East and North Africa, 2011–18

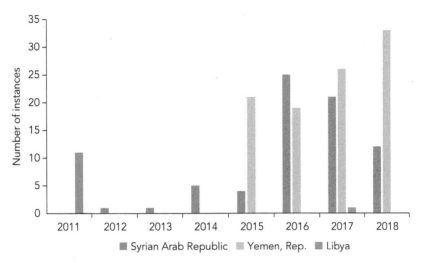

Source: Sowers, Weinthal, and Zawahri 2017. Data updated for water infrastructure targeted in Libya, the Syrian Arab Republic, and the Republic of Yemen, 2011–18. Overview of data and coding available at https://sites. nicholas.duke.edu/time/about-data/.
Note: Includes infrastructure related to drinking water, purification, irrigation, wastewater treatment, and sanitation. Data for Libya likely represent an underestimate given that few organizations are reporting from Libya on infrastructure destruction.

(UNOCHA 2020). News reports also highlighted that the drinkable water supply in Libya has decreased from approximately 149 to 101 water distribution canals because of their destruction as a result of the conflict (DW 2019).

Conflict and migration also have long-lasting cumulative impacts on water infrastructure and institutions. In Gaza, Iraq, Syria, the Republic of Yemen, and to a lesser extent Lebanon, decades of conflict, violence, blockades, and sanctions have generated long-lasting negative impacts on infrastructure and related services and livelihoods, and have hindered the rebuilding of water management infrastructure and institutions. As security situations deteriorate, experienced staff and personnel leave water ministries and utilities. This brain drain affects countries' ability to deliver services in the short term and also makes it much more difficult to rebuild institutions and infrastructure in the long term because of the lack of skilled professionals (ICRC 2015). Furthermore, in situations of protracted armed conflict, it becomes much more difficult to obtain the spare parts and consumables needed to maintain and operate water infrastructure. In turn, this accelerates even further the deterioration of infrastructure and services, in a downward vicious cycle.

DOES FORCED DISPLACEMENT CATALYZE CONFLICT AND TENSIONS OVER WATER?

Large-scale displacement is likely to increase population pressure on resources and services in host communities. Across the world, there is evidence of environmental degradation and resource pressures, including over water, among displaced populations and host communities (Maystadt et al. 2019; Maystadt et al. 2020). In Turkey, the Syrian refugee influx worsened environmental outcomes in provinces with poor-quality governance (Aksoy and Tumen 2021). Although there is evidence of increased pressures on resources and services, as also discussed in chapter 3, there is less evidence on how populations in refugee-receiving countries in the Middle East and North Africa react to refugees, including through violence (Alrababa'h et al. 2021). There is also less evidence indicating conflict and tensions over water following the refugee influx. Although there are localized reports of tensions among refugees and host communities around water access in the Middle East and North Africa, such as in Lebanon (UNDP 2019), overall evidence is far from complete.

For example, early in the Syrian crisis, water had been identified as a driver of community tension between Syrians and Jordanians. Surveys of host and refugee communities across the six northern governorates suggested that rising tensions in Jordanian host communities were linked to inadequate access to water (REACH 2014). Similarly, policy sources identified water as a source of vulnerability and tension between refugees and host communities in Jordan and Lebanon (Mercy Corps 2014; Baylouny and Klingseis 2018). However, subsequent research from Jordan and Lebanon suggests that concerns about the economic impact of refugees do not drive tensions among host communities, and that actually, humanitarian concerns for the well-being of the refugees prevail (Alrababa'h et al. 2021). This also seems to apply to IDPs, which in Syria were not perceived as driving tensions over resources and services (Fröhlich 2016). In this context, continued monitoring of social tensions and perceptions among refugees and host communities is critical to provide understanding of changes in social stability and dynamics (UNDP 2019).

LOOKING AHEAD: SOARING DEMAND, CLIMATE CHANGE, AND THE CHANGING NATURE OF CONFLICT

This report examines historical evidence linking water and conflict; however, the changing nature of both water and conflict also requires consideration of what the future might hold, with the understanding that the past may not always be the best predictor of the future. At present, the region's growing demands for water have made it a global hot spot of unsustainable water use and deteriorating water quality. Many countries in the Middle East and North Africa have significantly depleted and degraded their freshwater resources, with unsustainable volumes of groundwater being withdrawn in several countries in the region (World Bank 2017a).

This fragile water situation is colliding with climate change, which is expected to further change the face of water, leading to more variable and scarce water resources. In economic terms, climate change-induced water scarcity could reduce economic growth by 5 to 6 percent compared with current levels in some countries in the region (Taheripour et al. 2020). As economies shrink because of water scarcity, demand for labor could drop by more than 10 percent in some countries, with agricultural livelihoods dependent on water expected to suffer the most (Taheripour et al. 2020). Although the social consequences of these changes cannot be predicted, failure to prepare for their impacts would further strain an already fragile social, economic, and environmental system.

Conflict is also changing and becoming less traditional, blurring the lines between military and civilian. The targeting of water infrastructure described in the previous section is a clear example of this changing nature of conflict. However, other changes are taking place. For example, armed actors have become more numerous and more radical, with a myriad of shifting alliances fighting on many levels and on many fronts (McGoldrick 2015). More battles are being fought in densely populated urban areas with highly explosive weaponry and remotely piloted aircrafts (armed drones) or through cyberattacks. Finally, weapons and other harmful material such as chemical agents have become easier to obtain. As this trend continues, conflict is expected to lead to even more environmental degradation and destruction of critical infrastructure assets, with negative consequences for water security.

To conclude, addressing the changing nature of both water and conflict requires immediate action to increase the ability of people and economies to face this double challenge. As evidence of the disproportionate effects of climate change on countries and populations enduring conflict grows, so does the need to continue monitoring the dynamics described in this report in light of ever-changing conditions. In the Middle East and North Africa, decades of conflict have weakened people's ability to cope with water risks, increasing their vulnerability to climate change and thus creating additional conflict risk factors in places that lack strong governance and inclusive institutions, in a vicious cycle of insecurity and vulnerability. These dynamics are also at play in other parts of the world (box 2.5).

BOX 2.5: Combined Impact of Conflict and Climate-Related Water Risks: Evidence from Lake Chad

The Lake Chad region faces a combination of multidimensional risks related to conflict, forced displacement, climate change, and transboundary water management, among other factors. Lake Chad is a large transboundary lake shared between Cameroon, Chad, Niger, and Nigeria. From 2014 onward, as Boko Haram's violent activity spread from Nigeria into Cameroon, Chad, and Niger, the Lake Chad region experienced a humanitarian crisis and a large influx of internally displaced people and refugees.

However, even before the recent Boko Haram crisis, the Lake Chad region represented the poorest and most marginalized part of the riparian countries. Delivery of basic social services (including water, education, health, infrastructure, and electricity) in the vicinity of Lake Chad is poor, especially in the rural areas. As countries exploited the lake's resources, failure to cooperate over the shared freshwater resources contributed to the shrinking of the lake. This has forced ethnically diverse pastoralist communities from Niger and other riparian countries to move further south (World Bank 2016). This water-related displacement has heightened conflict over scarce resources among ethnic groups, many of which are armed. In fragile contexts in which armed and violent groups operate, these tensions could trigger further conflicts among riparian inhabitants in the Lake Chad region.

Climate change is further straining this situation, with reports of changes in the timing and amount of rainfall leading to loss of productivity of the rain-dependent agricultural areas (World Bank 2020). Temperatures in the region are rising one and a half times faster than the global average (Vivekananda et al. 2019). The population in the Lake Chad region is caught in a conflict–climate risk trap, in which violent conflict between state security forces and armed opposition groups, poor governance, and failure to cooperate have undermined communities' ability to cope and adapt to climate change (Vivekananda et al. 2019).

CONCLUSIONS

Through interviews and analysis of case studies and event data, this chapter suggests that water risks are more often related to cooperation than to conflict, both at the domestic and international levels. Noting the complex nature of the water, conflict, and cooperation nexus, the chapter furthermore suggests that cooperation and conflict often coexist. In addition, the evidence cautions against identifying forced displacement as a key intermediate variable linking water risks with conflict. As suggested in volume 1 of *Ebb and Flow*, causal relationships between water risks and human mobility cannot be generalized (Zaveri et al. 2021).

Although the chapter cautions against conjectures of large-scale forced displacement and conflict caused by water risks, it also highlights a set of concerning trends at the interface of water, forced displacement, and conflict. First, the chapter identifies situations in which failure to provide water services and support water-related livelihoods in the face of scarcity has induced small-scale movement of people, with examples from Iraq and Libya. Second, the chapter highlights how water policies, such as poorly planned irrigation expansion in dry areas and politicized access to land and water resources, can exacerbate vulnerability to water risks and climate change. In the case of Syria, this significantly contributed to additional hardships for rural Syrians, some of whom had to abandon their lands during the long drought of 2007. Third, the chapter shows concerning data suggesting that water is a victim of conflict, with instances of targeting of water infrastructure rising. Finally, the chapter highlights how the changing nature of water paired with the changing nature of conflict suggests that the future nexus of water, conflict, and forced displacement might look very different from the past.

NOTE

1. Note that 1 ton is equal to 1,000 kilograms; based on data from the United States Department of Agriculture Foreign Agricultural Service (https://apps.fas.usda.gov /psdonline/app/index.html#/app/home).

REFERENCES

Adams, C., T. Ide, J. Barnett, and A. Detges. 2018. "Sampling Bias in Climate–Conflict Research." *Nature Climate Change* 8 (3): 200–203.

Aksoy, C. G., and S. Tumen. 2021. "Local Governance Quality and the Environmental Cost of Forced Migration." *Journal of Development Economics* 149: 102603.

Al-Mudaffar Fawzi, N., K. P. Goodwin, B. A. Mahdi, and M. L. Stevens. 2016. "Effects of Mesopotamian Marsh (Iraq) Desiccation on the Cultural Knowledge and Livelihood of Marsh Arab Women." *Ecosystem Health and Sustainability* 2 (3): e01207.

Alrababa'h, A., A. Dillon, S. Williamson, J. Hainmueller, D. Hangartner, and J. Weinstein. 2021. "Attitudes toward Migrants in a Highly Impacted Economy: Evidence from the Syrian Refugee Crisis in Jordan." *Comparative Political Studies* 54 (1): 33–76.

Ash, K., and N. Obradovich. 2020. "Climatic Stress, Internal Migration, and Syrian Civil War Onset." *Journal of Conflict Resolution* 64 (1): 3–31.

Aw-Hassan, A., F. Rida, R. Telleria, and A. Bruggeman. 2014. "The Impact of Food and Agricultural Policies on Groundwater Use in Syria." *Journal of Hydrology* 513: 204–15.

Barnes, J. 2009. "Managing the Waters of Ba'th Country: The Politics of Water Scarcity in Syria." *Geopolitics* 14 (3): 510–30.

Baylouny, A. M, and S. J. Klingseis. 2018. "Water Thieves or Political Catalysts? Syrian Refugees in Jordan and Lebanon." *Middle East Policy* 25 (1): 104–23.

Bernauer, T., and T. Böhmelt. 2020. "International Conflict and Cooperation over Freshwater Resources." *Nature Sustainability* 3 (5): 350–56.

Bernauer, T., T. Böhmelt, H. Buhaug, N. P. Gleditsch, T. Tribaldos, E. B. Weibust, and G. Wischnath. 2012. "Water-Related Intrastate Conflict and Cooperation (WARICC): A New Event Dataset." *International Interactions: Empirical and Theoretical Research in International Relations* 38 (4): 529–45.

Böhmelt, T., T. Bernauer, H. Buhaug, N. P. Gleditsch, T. Tribaldos, and G. Wischnath. 2014. "Demand, Supply, and Restraint: Determinants of Domestic Water Conflict and Cooperation." *Global Environmental Change* 29: 337–48.

Breisinger, C., T. Zhu, P. Al Riffai, G. Nelson, R. Robertson, J. Funes, and D. Verner. 2013. "Economic Impacts of Climate Change in Syria." *Climate Change Economics* 4 (1): 1350002.

Buhaug, H. 2010. "Climate Not to Blame for African Civil Wars." *Proceedings of the National Academy of Sciences* 107 (38): 16477–82.

Cammett, M., and L. M. MacLean. 2014. *The Politics of Non-State Welfare.* Ithaca, NY: Cornell University Press.

Damania, R., S. Desbureaux, M. Hyland, A. Islam, S. Moore, A.-S. Rodella, J. Russ, and E. Zaveri. 2017. *Uncharted Waters: The New Economics of Water Scarcity and Variability.* Washington, DC: World Bank.

Daoudy, M. 2020. *The Origins of the Syrian Conflict: Climate Change and Human Security.* Cambridge: Cambridge University Press.

De Châtel, F. 2014. "The Role of Drought and Climate Change in the Syrian Uprising: Untangling the Triggers of the Revolution." *Middle Eastern Studies* 50 (4): 521–35.

De Stefano, L., P. Edwards, L. De Silva, and A. T. Wolf. 2010. "Tracking Cooperation and Conflict in International Basins: Historic and Recent Trends." *Water Policy* 12 (6): 871–84.

Döring, S. 2020. "From Bullets to Boreholes: A Disaggregated Analysis of Domestic Water Cooperation in Drought-Prone Regions." *Global Environmental Change* 65: 102147.

DW (Deutsche Welle). 2019. "The Specter of the Drinking Water Crisis Threatens Libya." DW, July 7, Libya.

Feitelson, E., and A. Tubi. 2017. "A Main Driver or an Intermediate Variable? Climate Change, Water and Security in the Middle East." *Global Environmental Change* 44: 39–48.

Fröhlich, C. J. 2016. "Climate Migrants as Protestors? Dispelling Misconceptions about Global Environmental Change in Pre-Revolutionary Syria." *Contemporary Levant* 1 (1): 38–50.

Gleick, P. H. 2014. "Water, Drought, Climate Change, and Conflict in Syria." *Weather, Climate, and Society* 6 (3): 331–40.

Gleick, P. H. 2019. "Water as a Weapon and Casualty of Armed Conflict: A Review of Recent Water-Related Violence in Iraq, Syria, and Yemen." *Wiley Interdisciplinary Reviews: Water* 6 (4): e1351.

Grynkewich, A. G. 2008. "Welfare as Warfare: How Violent Non-State Groups Use Social Services to Attack the State." *Studies in Conflict and Terrorism* 31 (4): 350–70.

Guiu, R. 2020. *When Canals Run Dry: Displacement Triggered by Water Stress in the South of Iraq*. Internal Displacement Monitoring Centre, Social Inquiry, and Norwegian Refugee Council. https://www.internal-displacement.org /sites/default/files/publications/documents/202002-iraq-slow-onset-report .pdf.

Haseeb, M. 2020. "Resources Scarcity and Cooperation: Job Market Paper." https://warwick.ac.uk/fac/soc/economics/staff/mhaseeb/jmp_haseeb.pdf.

Hsiang, S. M., M. Burke, and E. Miguel. 2013. "Quantifying the Influence of Climate on Human Conflict." *Science* 341 (6151): 1235367.

Human Rights Watch. 2019. *Basra Is Thirsty: Iraq's Failure to Manage the Water Crisis*. https://www.hrw.org/sites/default/files/report_pdf/iraq0719_web.pdf.

ICRC (International Committee of the Red Cross). 2015. *Urban Services During Protracted Armed Conflict: A Call for a Better Approach to Assisting Affected People*. Geneva: ICRC. https://www.icrc.org/sites/default/files/topic /file_plus_list/4249_urban_services_during_protracted_armed_conflict.pdf.

Ide, T., M. R. Lopez, C. Fröhlich, and J. Scheffran. 2020. "Pathways to Water Conflict during Drought in the MENA Region." *Journal of Peace Research* 58 (3): 568–82.

IOM (International Organization for Migration). 2012. *IOM Iraq Special Report: Water Scarcity*. Geneva: IOM. https://reliefweb.int/sites/reliefweb.int /files/resources/Water%20Scaricity.pdf.

IOM (International Organization for Migration). 2017. *IOM Middle East and North Africa: Regional Strategy 2017–2020*. Cairo: IOM Regional Office for the Middle East and North Africa. https://publications.iom.int/system/files /pdf/mena_regional_stategy.pdf.

IOM (International Organization for Migration). 2019. *Assessing Water Shortage-Induced Displacement in Missan, Muthanna, Thi-Qar, and Basra*. Geneva: IOM. https://displacement.iom.int/reports/iraq-%E2%80%93 -assessing-water-shortage-induced-displacement-southern-iraq-4-april-2019.

IOM (International Organization for Migration). 2020. *Libya IDP and Returnee Report: Mobility Tracking, Round 31, May–June 2020*. IOM Displacement Tracking Matrix. Geneva: IOM.

IOM (International Organization for Migration) and Deltares. 2020. *Water Quantity and Water Quality in Central and South Iraq: A Preliminary Assessment in the Context of Displacement Risk*. Geneva: IOM. https://iraq .iom.int/publications/water-quantity-and-water-quality-central-and-south -iraq-preliminary-assessment-context.

Jägerskog, A. 2018. "Are There Limits to Environmental Peacebuilding? A Critical Reflection on Water Cooperation in the Jordan Basin." In *Routledge Handbook on Environmental Conflict and Peacebuilding*, edited by A. Swain and J. Öjendal. London: Routledge.

Kelley, C. P., S. Mohtadi, M. A. Cane, R. Seager, and Y. Kushnir. 2015. "Climate Change in the Fertile Crescent and Implications of the Recent Syrian Drought." *Proceedings of the National Academy of Sciences* 112 (11): 3241–6.

Koubi, V. 2019. "Climate Change and Conflict." *Annual Review of Political Science* 22: 343–60.

Mach, K. J., and C. M. Kraan. 2021. "Science–Policy Dimensions of Research on Climate Change and Conflict." *Journal of Peace Research* 58 (1): 168–76.

Mach, K. J., C. M. Kraan, W. N. Adger, H. Buhaug, M. Burke, J. D. Fearon, C. B. Field, C. S. Hendrix, J.-F. Maystadt, J. O'Loughlin, P. Roessler, J. Scheffran, K. A. Schultz, and N. von Uexkull. 2019. "Climate as a Risk Factor for Armed Conflict." *Nature* 571 (7764): 193–7.

Maystadt, J.-F., K. Hirvonen, A. Mabiso, and J. Vandercasteelen. 2019. "Impacts of Hosting Forced Migrants in Poor Countries." *Annual Review of Resource Economics* 11 (1): 439–59.

Maystadt, J.-F., V. Mueller, J. Van Den Hoek, and S. Van Weezel. 2020. "Vegetation Changes Attributable to Refugees in Africa Coincide with Agricultural Deforestation." *Environmental Research Letters* 15 (4): 044008.

McGoldrick, C. 2015. "The State of Conflicts Today: Can Humanitarian Action Adapt?" *International Review of the Red Cross* 97 (900): 1179–208.

Mercy Corps. 2014. *Tapped Out: Water Scarcity and Refugee Pressures in Jordan.* https://www.mercycorps.org/research-resources/jordan-water-scarcity-refugees.

Morgan, M. G. 2014. "Use (and Abuse) of Expert Elicitation in Support of Decision Making for Public Policy." *Proceedings of the National Academy of Sciences* 111 (20): 7176–84.

Nie, Z., X. Yang, and Q. Tu. 2020. "Resource Scarcity and Cooperation: Evidence from a Gravity Irrigation System in China." *World Development* 135: 105035.

Norwegian Refugee Council. 2018. *Basra Fact Finding Mission Report #2.* https://reliefweb.int/sites/reliefweb.int/files/resources/NRC_2ndBasraMission%20Report_FINAL_9Oct.pdf.

REACH. 2014. *Access to Water and Tensions in Jordanian Communities Hosting Syrian Refugees: Thematic Assessment Report.* https://reliefweb.int/sites/reliefweb.int/files/resources/REACH_JOR_Report_WaterandTensionsinJordanianCommunitiesHostingSyrianRefugees.pdf.

Ruggeri, A., T.-I. Gizelis, and H. Dorussen. 2011. "Events Data as Bismarck's Sausages? Intercoder Reliability, Coders' Selection, and Data Quality." *International Interactions* 37 (3): 340–61.

Sadoff, C. W., E. Borgomeo, and D. de Waal. 2017. *Turbulent Waters: Pursuing Water Security in Fragile Contexts.* Washington, DC: World Bank.

Selby, J., O. S. Dahi, C. Fröhlich, and M. Hulme. 2017. "Climate Change and the Syrian Civil War Revisited." *Political Geography* 60: 232–44.

Solow, A. R. 2013. "A Call for Peace on Climate and Conflict." *Nature* 497 (7448): 179–80.

Sowers, J. L., E. Weinthal, and N. Zawahri. 2017. "Targeting Environmental Infrastructures, International Law, and Civilians in the New Middle Eastern Wars." *Security Dialogue* 48 (5): 410–30.

Taheripour, F., W. E. Tyner, E. Sajedinia, A. Aguiar, M. Chepeliev, E. Corong, C. Z. de Lima, and I. Haqiqi. 2020. *Water in the Balance.* Washington, DC: World Bank.

UNDP (United Nations Development Programme). 2019. *UNDP and ARK, Regular Perceptions Survey of Social Tensions throughout Lebanon, Wave VI (August 2019).* https://data2.unhcr.org/en/documents/details/71599.

UNOCHA (United Nations Office for the Coordination of Humanitarian Affairs). 2020. *2020 Humanitarian Response Monitoring: Periodic Monitoring Report (Jan-May 2020) Libya.* https://reliefweb.int/sites/reliefweb.int/files/resources/libya_hrp_2020_pmr.pdf.

Verner, D. 2011. *Syria Rural Development in a Changing Climate: Increasing Resilience of Income, Well-Being, and Vulnerable Communities.* Report No. 60765-SY–MENA. Washington, DC: World Bank.

Vivekananda, J., M. Wall, F. Sylvestre, and C. Nagarajanadelphi. 2019. *Shoring Up Stability: Addressing Climate and Fragility Risks in the Lake Chad Region.* Berlin: Adelphi. https://www.adelphi.de/en/publication/shoring-stability.

Ward, C., and S. Ruckstuhl. 2017. *Water Scarcity, Climate Change and Conflict in the Middle East: Securing Livelihoods, Building Peace.* London: Bloomsbury Publishing.

Weinthal, E., J. J. Troell, and M. Nakayama, eds. 2014. *Water and Post-conflict Peacebuilding.* Abingdon, Oxon: Routledge.

Wodon, Q., A. Liverani, G. Joseph, and N. Bougnoux, eds. 2014. *Climate Change and Migration: Evidence from the Middle East and North Africa.* Washington, DC: World Bank.

Wolf, A. T. 1998. "Conflict and Cooperation along International Waterways." *Water Policy* 1 (2): 251–65.

Wolf, A. T. 1999. "Water Wars and Water Reality: Conflict and Cooperation along International Waterways." In *Environmental Change, Adaptation, and Security,* edited by S. Lonergan, 251–65. Dordrecht: Springer.

Wolf, A. T. 2007. "Shared Waters: Conflict and Cooperation." *Annual Review of Environment and Resources* 32: 241–69.

Wolf, A. T., S. B. Yoffe, and M. Giordano. 2003. "International Waters: Identifying Basins at Risk." *Water Policy* 5 (1): 29–60.

World Bank. 2016. *Forced Displacement by the Boko Haram Conflict in the Lake Chad Region.* Washington, DC: World Bank.

World Bank. 2017a. *Beyond Scarcity: Water Security in the Middle East and North Africa.* Middle East and North Africa Development Report. Washington, DC: World Bank.

World Bank. 2017b. *Forcibly Displaced: Toward a Development Approach Supporting Refugees, the Internally Displaced, and Their Hosts.* Washington, DC: World Bank.

World Bank. 2017c. *The Toll of War: The Economic and Social Consequences of the Conflict in Syria.* Washington, DC: World Bank.

World Bank. 2020. *Lake Chad Region Recovery and Development Project (PROLAC).* Project Appraisal Document. Washington, DC: World Bank.

Zaveri, E., J. Russ, A. Khan, R. Damania, E. Borgomeo, and A. Jägerskog. 2021. *Ebb and Flow: Volume 1. Water, Migration, and Development.* Washington, DC: World Bank.

Zeitoun, M., and J. Warner. 2006. "Hydro-Hegemony: A Framework for Analysis of Transboundary Water Conflicts." *Water Policy* 8: 435–60.

CHAPTER THREE

LEAST PROTECTED, MOST AFFECTED

I am very concerned that water shortage will happen in Jordan. Since I arrived in Mafraq water cuts have happened constantly.

—Name withheld, Syrian refugee, Mafraq, Jordan, September 2020

COVID-19 has greatly affected my life . . . my family's expenditure on detergents, soaps, and sanitizers has doubled.

—Name withheld, Syrian refugee, southern Marka (Amman), Jordan, September 2020

KEY HIGHLIGHTS

- Access to safe drinking water is a daily struggle for millions of forcibly displaced Iraqis, Libyans, Palestinians, Syrians, and Yemenis, and for international migrants, heightening public health risks.

- Access to water and hygiene is critical both for containing COVID-19 (coronavirus) and for lowering its immediate impact; however, it comes at a cost for vulnerable forcibly displaced households. For this reason, access to safe drinking water among forcibly displaced and international migrant populations has declined following the outbreak of the COVID-19 pandemic.

- Beyond water access, risks related to water resources such as scarcity and floods threaten the lives and livelihoods of forcibly displaced people and risk undermining humanitarian and development responses.

- Although forced displacement is placing an unplanned burden on the water services of host communities, regional experiences suggest that empowering and working through local governments helps to adapt and expand coverage.

- Improved data collection and understanding of the characteristics and needs of forcibly displaced people are needed to inform long-term water policy responses.

INTRODUCTION

This chapter characterizes forcibly displaced populations and examines where they live and the type of water challenges they face, including in the context of the COVID-19 pandemic. Given the high level of informality and high number of people living in makeshift camps and informal settlements, it is difficult to provide a comprehensive and generalizable view of the water challenges faced by forcibly displaced persons. This chapter attempts to identify some of these challenges through qualitative interviews with forcibly displaced persons in Jordan and Lebanon and displacement data sets and surveys from the United Nations High Commissioner for Refugees (UNHCR), the International Organization for Migration (IOM), and the United Nations Relief and Works Agency for Palestine Refugees in the Near East (UNRWA).

The chapter shows that access to water remains a priority humanitarian need for forcibly displaced people, with millions struggling every day to access water of sufficient quantity and quality to meet their daily requirements across the Middle East and North Africa. When drinking water is available, its poor quality and price mean that access to safe drinking water for forcibly displaced populations and host communities is still compromised. Although access to water services is a major challenge, water resource scarcity and water risks, in particular floods, are also key determinants of vulnerability. Floods threaten the lives and livelihoods of forcibly displaced persons, while water scarcity often prevents them from returning to their place of origin and sustaining their livelihoods in the long term.

WHO ARE THE FORCIBLY DISPLACED POPULATIONS AND THEIR HOST COMMUNITIES?

About 21 million people were living in forced displacement in the Middle East and North Africa at the end of 2020. An additional 5 million people originating from the Middle East and North Africa fled to countries outside the region, including Turkey and countries in the European Union. Three distinct groups are included under this total (for definitions see appendix A): (a) 2.2 million refugees and asylum seekers from the region hosted in countries of the Middle East and North Africa; (b) 12.4 million internally displaced persons owing to conflict and violence; and (c) 5.6 million Palestinian refugees registered with UNRWA.

The Syrian Arab Republic and the Republic of Yemen stand out for the scale of forced displacement. The Republic of Yemen is the worst humanitarian crisis worldwide, with more than 80 percent of the population requiring some form of assistance, 20 million facing food insecurity, and 14 million requiring urgent humanitarian intervention (UNHCR 2020). As the Syrian crisis enters its tenth year, its levels of forced displacement remain the highest in the world, with more than 6.5 million refugees and asylum seekers and about the same number of internally displaced persons (IDPs) (figure 3.1).

Lebanon, Jordan, and the West Bank and Gaza host many refugees. Approximately 30 percent of the population in the West Bank are refugees (1,047,990 people), most of whom (70 percent) live outside of refugee camps. In Gaza, approximately 73 percent of the population are refugees (1,570,295 people), of whom 600,000 live in refugee camps. There are 8 refugee camps in Gaza and 19 in the West Bank. Overall, about 8 percent of Palestinians live in refugee camps in the West Bank and Gaza (UNEP 2020), and about 50 percent of the Palestinian population is registered with UNRWA, as shown in figure 3.2. In Jordan and Lebanon, there are more than 700,000 and almost 1 million Syrian refugees, respectively, in addition to Palestinian refugees who have been in protracted forced displacement for decades (2.3 million in Jordan, almost half a million in Lebanon). The Arab Republic of Egypt is also a destination country, with refugees arriving from across the Middle East and East Africa. There are around 259,000

FIGURE 3.1: Countries and Economies of Origin of Forced Displacement, 2020

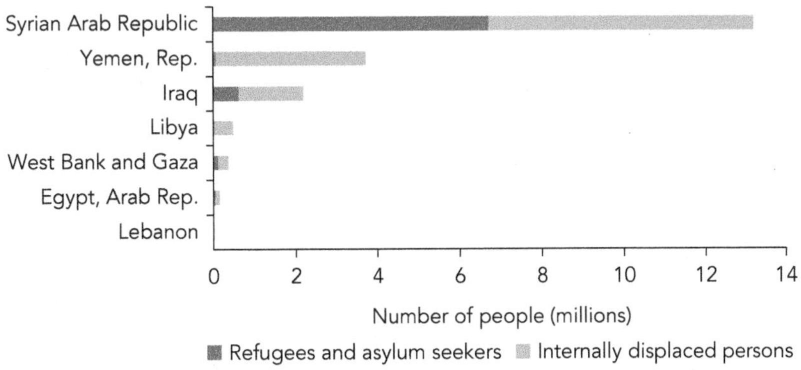

Source: World Bank using data from UNHCR.

FIGURE 3.2: Number of Refugees, Asylum Seekers, and Palestinian Refugees Hosted, by Country and Economy, 2020

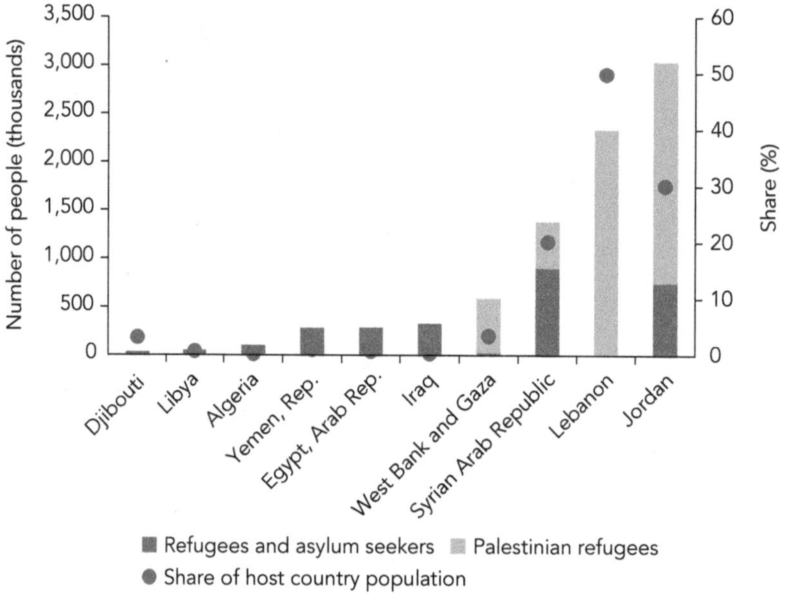

Source: World Bank using data from UNHCR.

registered refugees and asylum seekers from 58 different countries: half are from Syria (130,000), followed by Sudan (49,000), South Sudan (20,000), Eritrea (19,000), and Ethiopia (16,000).

Although these numbers reflect a stark reality, they do not fully reflect the specific challenges faced by forcibly displaced individuals, especially those from socially excluded groups and marginalized communities. In the context of forced displacement, individuals might face both external and internal factors that compromise their agency and access to services. External factors include country of origin, restrictions on owning land or a house, and location of settlement, while internal factors include lack of personal endowments or agency because of societal norms, identity, or disabilities (World Bank 2018a). For water security, this translates to lower levels of water access, but also less participation in decision-making when it comes to the use and allocation of water within the household or community. Although data on social inclusion in the context of forced displacement are scarce, there is evidence of individuals and communities being disadvantaged or excluded from access to services and decision-making, including in relation to water, because of disability and their identity, in particular as it relates to gender.

Among forcibly displaced people, individuals with disability status are the first group facing specific challenges and vulnerabilities. UNHCR estimates that an average 4 percent of refugees and asylum seekers in the region have disability status (figure 3.3) (UNHCR 2019a). Underidentification of persons with disability is a common concern, especially in conflict-affected contexts, so the data in figure 3.3 should be considered with caution and are most likely an underestimation of the overall share of persons with disability among the region's refugee and asylum seeker population. This also explains the difference between this estimate and that of the *World Report on Disability*, which suggests that 15 percent of the world's population has moderate or severe disability (WHO and World Bank 2011).

Single women, widows, and children in households headed by a woman are a second group of forcibly displaced individuals facing heightened risks and constraints. Almost one in every three households in Syria is headed by a woman (UNFPA 2014), with similar shares found across Syrian refugee households in Jordan (CARE International 2016). In situations of protracted armed conflict and forced displacement, women and girls are most exposed to adversity, and many of the water risks they face are heightened. Women face a number of water risks, including higher rates of gender-based violence exacerbated by the inadequate access to water and sanitation facilities and the impacts of water shocks on livelihoods and well-being (for example, through reduced food production).

FIGURE 3.3: Share of Refugees and Asylum Seekers with Disability Status, by Country in the Middle East and North Africa, 2019

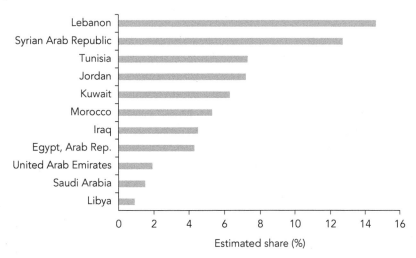

Source: UNHCR 2019a.
Note: The numbers in this figure show the share of persons based only on the disability codes entered by UNHCR staff at the time of registration (and during continuous registration processes), or other staff and partners during the courses of protection monitoring and interventions, and do not include persons with chronic medical conditions, mental illness, and other sources of registration (that is, registered by entities other than UNHCR). UNHCR's disability codes are based on the following definition: persons with disabilities include those who have long-term physical, mental, intellectual, or sensory impairments which in interaction with various barriers may hinder their full and effective participation in society on an equal basis with others.

Finally, although the chapter mostly describes the water challenges faced by forcibly displaced individuals and host communities, it is also important to identify those left behind. These include family members of migrants and forcibly displaced persons who stay behind in the place of origin, as well as people who are not able to move because of barriers to migration and spatial inequalities. In the first case, they can be trapped because conflict conditions prevent them from embarking on often perilous journeys to cross international borders. In countries not in conflict, immobility can also arise from spatial inequalities. Compared with the rest of the world, people in the Middle East and North Africa move less within their countries. On average, 14 percent of the region's people living in countries not affected by fragility have moved from their places of birth, compared with an average of 28 percent elsewhere (World Bank 2020a). Spatial inequalities, including in access to services, are likely to increase if there are barriers to labor flows between regions and benefits do not spill over to less fortunate regions.

WHERE DO THE FORCIBLY DISPLACED POPULATIONS LIVE AND WHAT WATER RISKS DO THEY FACE?

Most of the forcibly displaced populations live in towns and cities, in either formal or informal settlements. In the highly urbanized Middle East and North Africa, an estimated 80 to 90 percent of forcibly displaced persons live in cities, significantly above the global average of 60 percent (World Bank 2017a). This report broadly categorizes forced displacement settings and related water challenges into three distinct types: camps, cities and informal settlements heavily affected by conflict damage in countries of origin, and cities and informal settlements in countries of arrival (figure 3.4).

Camps

Water issues in camps hosting refugees and internally displaced persons vary widely depending on camp type and location. Camps can be broadly categorized into (a) open "urbanized" camps close to cities where residents are able to move in and out in search of livelihoods and other water sources (for example, Zaatari in Jordan, UNRWA camps in the West Bank and Gaza) and (b) closed camps in remote, inaccessible locations distant from cities and where movement in and out of the camps is restricted (for example, Tindouf in Algeria, Al-Hol camp in Syria) (World Bank 2017a).

FIGURE 3.4: Three Displacement Settings and Related Characteristics

Camps	Cities and informal settlements in country of origin	Cities and informal settlements in country of arrival
• Closed camps in remote areas (e.g., Al-Hol, Syrian Arab Republic) • Open urbanized camps close to cities (e.g., Zaatari, Jordan)	• Heavily affected by conflict damage • Water systems largely nonfunctional • Example: IDPs, returnees and trapped populations in Aleppo, Misrata, Mosul, Gaza, Sanaa	• Makeshift camps in marginal areas unconnected to water systems • Unplanned burden on water systems • Example: Refugees and international migrants in Bekaa Valley, Mafraq, Erbil

Source: World Bank.
Note: IDPs = internally displaced persons.

Water risks faced by forcibly displaced persons in these two types of camps can be quite different.

In easier-to-access "open" camps closer to urban areas and cities, forcibly displaced persons tend to experience levels of access to water services and water-related livelihoods comparable to those of their host community. For example, access to improved water in camps hosting Palestinians registered as refugees with UNRWA[1] in the West Bank is high and matches the levels in urban and rural areas. In the West Bank, there are no significant differences in access to water services between Palestinians living in camps and those living outside of camps (figure 3.5). In Gaza, where the situation remains at crisis level, there are at least 1,460,315 Palestinian refugees (UNRWA 2019) whose water issues are similar to the ones faced by most inhabitants having to buy desalinated water from unregulated water vendors (World Bank 2018b). The observation that forcibly displaced persons in urbanized camps face similar water-related issues to their host communities also applies to Palestinian refugees under UNRWA's mandate in Lebanon (box 3.1 on the Shatila refugee camp) and some Syrian refugees in some camps in Jordan, where the situation has recently improved (box 3.2 on the Zaatari refugee camp). In some rare cases, forcibly displaced persons residing in camps might enjoy greater access to water services compared with their host community. For example, access to piped sewerage for Palestinian refugees living in open, urbanized camps in the West Bank and Gaza is greater than the access to piped sewerage enjoyed by the population in rural areas (World Bank 2018b), as shown in figure 3.5.

Forcibly displaced persons living in closed, remote camps typically face much greater challenges in accessing clean water and sanitation services.

FIGURE 3.5: **Access to Drinking Water and to Improved Unshared Sanitation Facilities by Area of Residence in West Bank and Gaza, Including Camps and Source of Water, 2014**

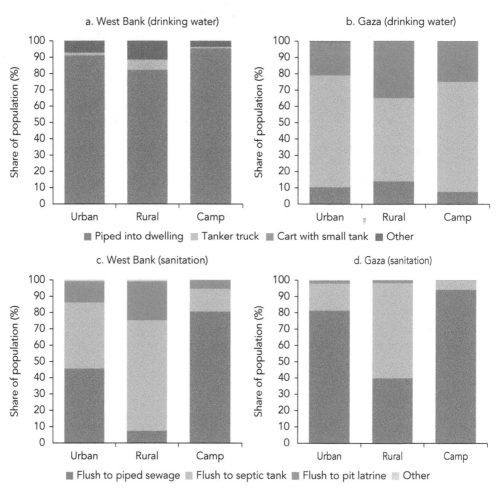

Source: World Bank 2018b

In Algeria, where about 100,000 refugees have been living in remote closed camps near Tindouf in southwest Algeria since 1975 (UNHCR 2016), water has been a key concern since the setting up of the camps. Current water supply infrastructure includes groundwater wells, reverse osmosis water treatment, and distribution networks to community points. Although some refugee households receive water from the distribution network, most still rely on water tankers and then store the water in private tanks. Although the water supply situation has improved over the past five years, Sahrawi refugees in Tindouf only receive 18 liters of potable water available per person per day on average (UNHCR 2016), which is below the 20 liters per person per

BOX 3.1: Water Challenges in the Shatila Refugee Camp, Beirut, Lebanon

The Shatila refugee camp was established for Palestinian refugees in 1949 in southern Beirut by the International Committee of the Red Cross (ICRC). Originally built for 3,000 people, the camp covers an area of 39,500 square meters and at first hosted around 500 tents. Exact figures for residents are hard to ascertain; however, one Shatila camp resident interviewed in summer 2020 as part of this study suggested that the total number of residents in the camp was 15,000 before 2011. In the nine years following the Syria Arab Republic crisis, the population has increased to about 30,000. Aside from natural growth from pre-2011 levels, the arrival of Syrian and 1,000 Palestinian refugees from Syria accounts for the population doubling. The tenfold increase in the camp's population since 1949 has taken place without any increase in the camp's land area (0.4 square kilometers) because camps cannot legally expand beyond their allotted space. This means that, unlike other refugee camps, the camp has expanded vertically rather than horizontally.

The dramatic population increase has placed considerable stress on water resources and services. Both Shatila's informal governing body, the Popular Committee, and the United Nations Relief and Works Agency for Palestine Refugees in the Near East have reported that the sewerage system functions poorly and the potential for cross-contamination between well water and the sewerage system is high, especially given the sandy soil that separates them (Khoury et al. 2016). Within the camp, there are four wells from which water is extracted, treated, and distributed by vendors. The wells consist of two public groundwater wells (35 and 40 meters deep) owned by the Popular Committee and two private wells (both 45 meters deep). Water from these wells is pumped directly into pipes that feed rooftop tanks and water vendors, of which there are 8 supplying 55 water shops. The well water is saline owing to the high salt content of Beirut's overpumped coastal aquifer. In some years, acute water shortages and aquifer overpumping have rendered the levels of total dissolved solids in many of Beirut's wells equivalent to that of seawater (around 37,500 milligrams per liter). Because of high demand, Shatila's withdrawals from these aquifers often exceed the rates of recharge—even in rainy seasons—causing a considerable amount of seawater intrusion. Given its location atop a large limestone reserve, Shatila also faces the added problem of pumping well water that is contaminated by high levels of calcium. Like much of Beirut, Shatila's residents have increasingly had to rely on desalination equipment. According to one camp resident interviewed as part of this study, about 50 percent of the water piped to the shops is desalinated for potability. A considerable number of camp residents thus use saline or calcified water for household use.

Source: Khoury et al. 2016 and qualitative semistructured interviews carried out by the West Asia-North Africa Institute for the World Bank Group.

BOX 3.2: A Syrian's Access to Water in the Zaatari Camp

The 33-year-old man came to the Zaatari camp in 2013 from Inkhil, a small village located north of the Dar'a governorate (80 kilometers from Jordan). He left the Syrian Arab Republic out of fear for his children's lives upon the destruction of his house. His last days in Syria were very difficult because he could access neither food nor water. He left with his wife and four children. He now lives in Zaatari and—since coming to Jordan—has had two more children. In Syria, he worked in agriculture. Water was never an issue in Syria in terms of quantity and cleanliness—the family drank directly from the tap and had no issues.

When he arrived at Zaatari, he was shocked by the lack of water and was not accustomed to conserving and using so much less. He owns a 2,000-liter tank that is filled every six days. It is enough for household use, but not for his plants. However, he thanks God for no longer having to stand in queues at communal tanks. At the end of 2018, the water network that had been under construction for years finally connected to his caravan, where water could now be piped directly. Before that, he had to fetch water—sometimes five times a day—often arguing with neighbors over water shares and leakage. While he was at work, his wife had to fetch the water and that was an ordeal. She could not stand among the men and she could not push her way through, meaning that his family often ended up with less water. That was until the families reached an agreement whereby they divided the water in proportion to the number of household members.

The water in Zaatari is free. He does not pay anything but he had to purchase a water filter to clean the water because he felt his water supplies were not clean enough. "Come see my plants, they are so thirsty. At the same time, I see water waste around the camp but have no way to harvest it for my plants. I wish I could get more water to water my simple plants (mint, parsley)," he said. He heard of water recycling programs around the camp and applied to them but has yet to hear back. His family uses the grey water produced from the filter for cleaning outside the caravan because it cannot be used for anything else. Currently, he is not working, though he used to take on labor jobs outside of the camp in agriculture and construction. His main goal is to save money for an eye operation for his daughter because she has a severe case that needs medical attention.

Source: Qualitative semistructured interviews carried out by the West Asia-North Africa Institute for the World Bank Group.

day recommended by the World Health Organization (WHO) needed to take care of basic hygiene and food hygiene.[2] In terms of drinking water quality, risks of microbial and chemical contamination are high, with reports of high levels of fluoride, chloride, nitrate, and sulfate in the camps' water supply (Vivar et al. 2016). Practicing good hand hygiene behaviors is also a challenge: among refugees in southwestern Algeria, the amount of bleach and soap produced in camp-based workshops is not enough to meet refugees' needs, meaning that only half of the humanitarian standard of 500 grams per person per month can be distributed (UNHCR 2016).

Forcibly displaced persons living in closed, remote camps also typically face greater flood risks. Camps for refugees and IDPs in Syria and the Republic of Yemen are at particular risk from flooding, as highlighted by recent events. For example, in 2018 and 2019, the Areesha and Al-Hol camps in Syria's Al-Hassakeh governorate were affected by severe flooding, which forced about 27,000 IDPs to relocate (IDMC and NRC 2020). In 2020, large parts of the Republic of Yemen were affected by flash floods causing an estimated 66,000 to 300,000 new displacements in less than three months, most of which were IDPs initially displaced by the conflict (IDMC and NRC 2020). Similarly, flood risks also affect refugees in Algeria, where camps are exposed to the risk of flash floods, which in 2015 affected at least 90,000 Sahrawi refugees (UNHCR 2015).

Persons with disabilities living in both types of camps often face greater difficulties in accessing water and sanitation services, particularly latrines. A 2018 disability assessment among Syrian refugees in three locations across Jordan suggests that households with persons with disabilities (that is, households with at least one member with disability) reported higher rates of latrine inaccessibility in camps compared with households with persons without disabilities (figure 3.6) (Humanity & Inclusion and iMMAP 2018). This suggests that even in camps with private latrines available (such as Zaatari), persons with disability can still struggle to use them because of various access challenges, the impact of which varies from person to person (such as slippery surface, small space inside, lack of handrails). Inaccessible latrines might result in persons with disability using shelters as bathrooms, resulting in unsanitary conditions and health risks (Arab Forum for the Rights of Persons with Disabilities 2016).

Women and children living in camps also face specific water-related challenges. In Gaza, lack of access to adequate sanitation services prevents women and girls from participating in other productive activities (such as attending school). In refugee camps in Jordan, Syrian women reported low levels of safety when collecting water from shared water points and fear of being physically attacked (United Nations and Partners 2016). The situation of women and children with ties to Islamic State suspects is of particular concern. Numerous reports from United Nations and humanitarian agencies suggest situations of desperate need for the nearly 65,000 people (of whom

FIGURE 3.6: Access to Services among Syrian Arab Republic Refugees in Three Locations in Jordan, by Household with Disability, 2018

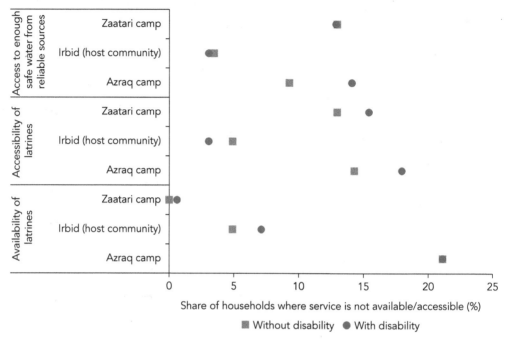

Source: Humanity & Inclusion and iMMAP 2018.
Note: Number of household/people surveyed: Azraq = 332 households (1,818 persons); Irbid = 445 households (2,620 persons); Zaatari = 382 households (1,942 persons).

about half are children under 12 years of age) held in the Al-Hol camp as of August 2020, who are facing water shortages and an ongoing outbreak of acute diarrhea, all in the context of the COVID-19 pandemic and limited or no available health care (MSF 2020; UNICEF 2020).

Cities and Informal Settlements in Country of Origin

The water security situation in cities and towns in the place of origin that are heavily affected by conflict damage is particularly dire. In northwestern Syria, 30 percent of IDPs living in informal settlements and makeshift camps identified access to water, sanitation, and hygiene (WASH) services as their first priority (UNOCHA 2019b). In Syria, sanitation needs are considerably higher among Syrian IDPs living in informal settlements compared to the rest of the population, with overcrowding, cleanliness, and protection concerns linked with substandard conditions of sanitation facilities frequently reported (UNOCHA 2019b). Across Syria, IDPs mostly rely on shared facilities, with 25 percent of IDPs sharing toilets with more than six people (REACH 2019). This is a particular challenge for IDPs with disabilities, who do not have access to appropriate sanitation facilities (UNOCHA 2019b).

A similar situation is reported for the Republic of Yemen, where more than half of the IDP and returnee population lacks access to adequate and sufficient quantities of drinking water (IOM 2019a). The latest round of IOM surveys suggests that 53 percent of IDP and returnee populations and 55 percent of refugee and migrant (non-Yemeni) populations lack access to an adequate and sufficient quantity of water. In addition, cholera affected water supplies in 96 percent of the country's governorates in 2020 (USAID 2020). Given that these surveys were carried out during the rainy season, it is likely that the share of people without access to drinking water might even be greater in the dry season. This limited access to even basic drinking water means that the need for drinking water, sanitation, and hygiene is the fourth mostly commonly reported priority need identified by IDPs and returnees, following food, access to income, and shelter and housing (figure 3.7).

Forcibly displaced persons in the Republic of Yemen also struggle with low access to sanitation services; 59 percent of IDP and returnee populations and 62 percent of refugee and international migrant populations do not have access to a safe and functioning latrine (IOM 2019b). In areas with

FIGURE 3.7: Primary Humanitarian Needs of IDPs and Returnees in the Republic of Yemen, 2019

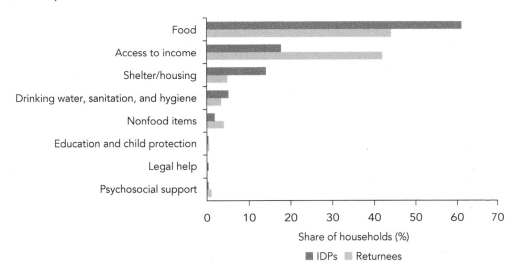

Source: IOM 2019a.
Note: IDPs = internally displaced persons. Total IDPs surveyed = 607,875 households (3,647,250 individuals). Total returnees surveyed = 213,427 households (1,280,562 individuals). Nonfood items include blankets, clothing, mattresses, fuel, and cooking utensils.

low access to sanitation services, the incidence of malnutrition and cholera is higher. This is aligned with district-specific assessments, which highlight IDPs' access constraints to sanitation in the Republic of Yemen (World Bank 2017b). Beyond water and sanitation access issues, water in the Republic of Yemen is also a main factor cited by IDPs and returnees as leading to the decline of their livelihoods and access to income-generating activities. Supply of water for agriculture is one of the most frequently reported factors needed to improve livelihoods, among both IDPs and host communities. For nonhost communities, lack of water for livestock emerges as a key obstacle to sustainable livelihoods.

Internally displaced persons and returnees in Iraq also face severe water challenges. Across Iraq, the number of people in need of WASH assistance includes approximately 600,000 IDPs (of whom about half reside in out-of-camp locations) and 1.06 million returnees; 14,724 people in highly vulnerable host communities; and more than 100,000 refugees in nine refugee camps and out-of-camp locations (UNOCHA 2019a). Of these, 317,663 people lack access to an improved water source, while 679,751 people lack access to sufficient quantities of water[3] (UNOCHA 2019a). In Iraq, lack of safe and adequate drinking water services prevents people from returning to their place of origin. IDP households cite lack of basic services, including water, at origin as the second most important reason preventing them from returning, after lack of job opportunities (IOM 2019c). When people do return, lack of water compromises their lives and livelihoods. In Iraq, around 35 percent of returnees reside in areas with critical water shortages (fewer than 75 percent of households having access to water) (IOM 2019c).

Tanker trucks often help fill the gap by providing access to water for forcibly displaced persons and returnees; however, this raises issues of water quality and affordability. As a result of the high reliance on water trucks and bottled water, IDPs and returnees often find water to be unaffordable. In Libya, where water trucks and water bottles are key water sources (figure 3.8), IDPs and returnees find water to be unaffordable in more than 50 percent of the country's municipalities (IOM 2020a).

Single women, widows, and children in female-headed households face heightened risks and constraints. In Syria, IDPs and returnee female-headed households have more difficulty affording a majority of hygiene items in comparison with female-headed households in Syrian host communities (UNOCHA 2019b). Among those left behind in Syria's government-controlled cities, women indicate that collecting water takes considerable time and effort, adding to their hardships (WFP 2018). In these areas, the share of female-headed households reporting not having continuous water supply is higher than among male-headed households (42 percent versus 35 percent), as is also the share of households not having access to drinking water for several days (53 percent versus 46 percent), according to survey data collected by Johns Hopkins Bloomberg School of Public

FIGURE 3.8: Main Sources of Water among IDPs, Returnees, International Migrants, and Host Communities in Libya, 2020

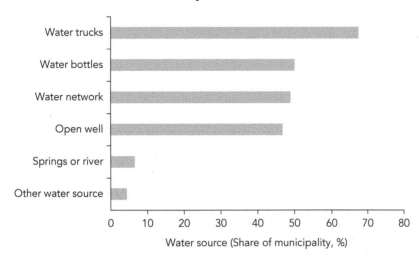

Source: IOM 2020a.
Note: Main sources of water (multiple choice) in use to meet needs of residents, including IDPs, host communities, and migrants (share of municipality). IDPs = internally displaced persons.

Health (Doocy and Lyles 2017). Although no major differences were reported between male- and female-headed households with regard to access to toilet facilities, female-headed households had lower access to hygiene and childcare products (Doocy and Lyles 2017). For instance, in Syria, affordability of baby diapers for female-headed households is an issue for 17 percent of returnees and 8 percent of IDPs, compared with less than 1 percent of host communities (UNOCHA 2019b). Although this section has focused on places of origin heavily affected by protracted armed conflict, some of these challenges are also faced by trapped populations in relatively more stable countries (box 3.3).

Cities and Informal Settlements in Country of Arrival

For millions of forcibly displaced persons living in informal settlements and cities in places of destination, availability of drinking water and sanitation services remains a major humanitarian need. In Libya, access to water is among the primary humanitarian needs of international migrants and refugees. Water, sanitation, and hygiene are regularly listed by migrants and refugees as a top priority following food, health services, and nonfood items (such as blankets, clothing, mattresses, fuel, and cooking utensils). The need for drinking water is particularly high in Libya's coastal *mantikas* (regions), where a large population of international migrants is present (Tripoli, Ejdabia, and Misrata, hosting 14 percent, 12 percent, and 10 percent of the country's international migrant and refugee population, respectively). About 26 percent of international migrants trapped in Libya report having insufficient water to drink and significant challenges accessing the public drinking water network, with 6 percent reporting never having access and 20 percent rarely having access (IOM 2020b). Given the lack of access to public drinking water supplies, these migrants use alternative drinking water sources, including bottled water (72 percent), while others rely on protected wells (30 percent), outdoor public taps (13 percent), or water trucks (12 percent) (IOM 2020b), which are often too expensive or unreliable to

BOX 3.3: Water Risks and Those Left Behind

In the Middle East and North Africa, people left behind typically live in lagging rural regions, and suffer disparity and deficiency in the quality of water services (World Bank 2020a). Coverage of improved drinking water and sanitation services is markedly lower in rural areas across the Middle East and North Africa, as shown in figure B3.3.1. People left behind also face greater water risks. Figure B3.3.2 shows that higher spatial inequality is associated with greater water risks.

FIGURE B3.3.1: Gaps in Networked Water Supply and Sanitation Services between Capital City and Other Areas

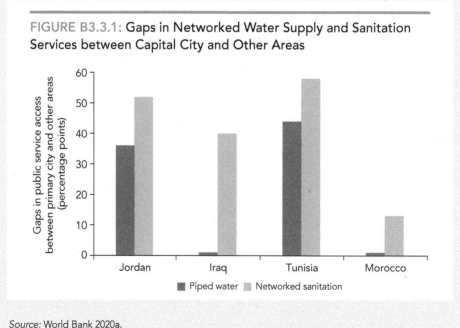

Source: World Bank 2020a.

box continues next page

BOX 3.3: Water Risks and Those Left Behind *continued*

FIGURE B3.3.2: Water Risks Are Associated with Higher Spatial Inequality in the Middle East and North Africa Region

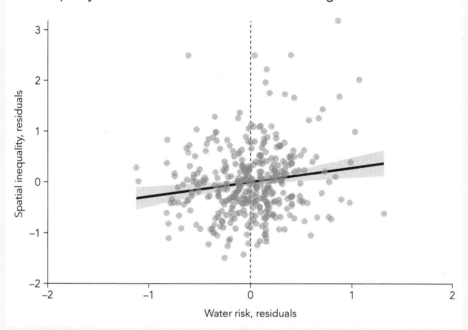

Source: World Bank 2020a.
Note: The figure shows residual-on-residual plots with 95 percent confidence intervals. The x-axis depicts the residuals from an ordinary least squares (OLS) regression on water risk from aqueduct data controlling for population, area, time to access nearest city, economic density, and country-fixed effects. The y-axis corresponds to mean log deviation of poverty rate as an indicator of inequality (Haughton and Khandker 2009) on the same controls. Each point is an administrative region corresponding to the lowest administrative area with poverty rates available. Most correspond to the first administrative level; Morocco and Lebanon are the second administrative level, province and district, respectively; and Jordan is the third administrative level (subdistrict). No data were available for the Gulf Cooperation Council countries, Libya, and the Syrian Arab Republic. Spatial inequality data from the Middle East and North Africa Poverty Database (MNAPOV), Team for Statistical Development, World Bank, and water risk data from the World Resources Institute's Aqueduct Water Risk Atlas (https://www.wri.org/resources/maps/aqueduct-water-risk-atlas).

Out-migration of family members and their remittances can help those left behind cope with some of these water risks. In Morocco, for example, Kuper et al. (2012) interviewed 300 farmers in the Tadia irrigation scheme and showed that 47 percent of the farmers with regular revenues from migrants installed a tube well versus 36 percent who did not benefit from such revenues. In the Republic of Yemen, households with no income rely on remittances from family and friends to acquire water (World Bank 2017b).

provide sufficient quantities of water. As shown in figure 3.9, one in four migrants does not have access to a regular supply of public drinking water, and only one-quarter of migrants report having daily access.

When water is available, it is often not safe for drinking, with refugees in cities and informal settlements across host countries facing significant challenges in accessing safe drinking water that is free from contaminants. In Lebanon, water to informal settlements hosting Syrian refugees is of poorer quality compared with that delivered to residents (WHO and UNICEF 2016). At least one-quarter of all refugee households in informal settlements are accessing very highly contaminated drinking water (WHO and UNICEF 2016). Compared with permanent residents, Syrian refugees living in informal settlements face much higher health risks with regard to *Escherichia coli* contamination of their water supply (figure 3.10). This poorer water quality to informal settlements is partly related to the low quality of the tanker-transported water. Figure 3.10 shows the deterioration in water quality that occurs within Syrian households in informal settlements, so that water supplies initially categorized as low risk become higher risk, often as a result of lack of adequate water storage facilities in the household or as a result of transport from the point of distribution (for example, springs) to the house for consumption. A similar situation is reported for Syrian refugees in cities and informal settlements in Jordan. According to UNHCR, 64 percent of Syrians in Jordan are identified as highly or severely vulnerable to WASH risks, largely driven by very high costs of securing drinking water supplies and hygiene items (UNHCR 2019b).

Refugees in informal settlements also struggle to access sanitation services. Syrian refugees in Lebanon are likely to lack access to a toilet (16 percent on average) compared with refugees in Jordan (5 percent), but

FIGURE 3.9: Share of International Migrant Population by Frequency of Access to Public Drinking Water Supply

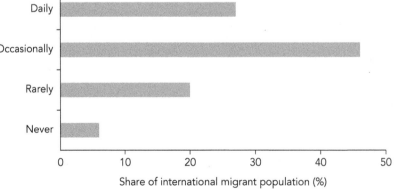

Share of international migrant population (%)

Source: IOM 2020b

FIGURE 3.10: **Percentage of Lebanese Households Exposed to** *E. coli* **at Point of Consumption and Distribution**

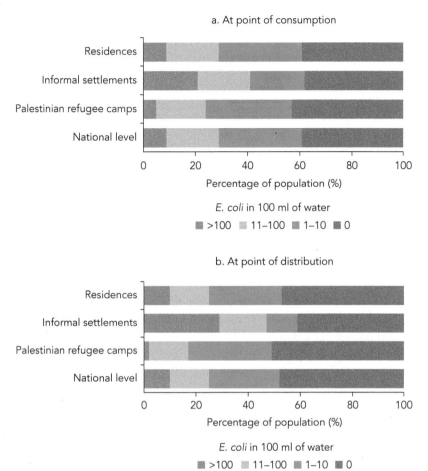

Source: WHO and UNICEF 2016.
Note: E. coli = Escherichia coli; 100 ml = a typical cup of drinking water; ml = milliliters.

most refugees in Lebanon do not have to share a toilet (figure 3.11). Only 28 percent have shared access, compared with nearly half (47 percent) of those living in Jordan (World Bank 2020b). In Jordan, Syrian refugees struggle to meet their hygiene expenditure. Hygiene expenditure per capita (including sanitary napkins, diapers, and personal care items) has a mean of 4.64 Jordanian dinars per month and a median of 2.37 Jordanian dinars per month. UNHCR survey data suggest that 40 percent of refugees living in four governorates (Amman, Irbid, Mafraq, and Zarqa) cannot afford to buy some basic hygiene items (sanitary napkins, diapers, and personal care items), while an additional 3.5 percent of the sample reported extreme WASH poverty and could not buy any of the basic items to meet their WASH needs (UNHCR 2019b). Access to basic hygiene items is also a

FIGURE 3.11: **Access to Sanitation Services for Syrian Refugees, by Host Country and Location, 2017**

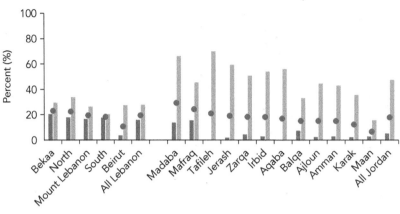

■ No access   ■ Shared access   ● Sanitation Deprivation Index

Source: World Bank 2020c.
Note: The Sanitation Deprivation Index is 0.7 × limited access + 0.3 × not private toilet.

challenge for IDPs in Syria, with 10 percent reporting not being able to afford them (UNOCHA 2019b).

In protracted refugee situations, women and girls are most exposed to adversity, and many of the water risks they face are heightened in informal settlements. Women face a number of water risks, including higher rates of gender-based violence exacerbated by inadequate access to water and sanitation facilities and the impacts of water deficits on livelihoods and well-being (for example, through reduced food production). The impact of these water risks is often exacerbated by cultural norms and internalized inequality. Among Syrian refugee women in Lebanon, lack of access to facilities for basic hygiene, including lack of drinking water and lack of access to feminine hygiene products, washing water, soap, and bathing facilities, are key factors contributing to poor reproductive health (Masterson et al. 2014). Among Syrian refugees in Lebanon, children are forced to work and they face hard working conditions, with girls less likely to receive water to drink at work compared with boys (Habib et al. 2019). In addition, the protracted humanitarian crisis and lack of services has exacerbated gender-based violence in all its forms, including sexual violence, intimate partner violence, and child marriage (UN Women 2020).

Finally, although there is no regionwide assessment of the flood risks faced by refugees and international migrants living in cities and informal settlements, country evidence suggests that flooding is a key determinant of vulnerability. Forcibly displaced persons often settle on land prone to water-related disasters, such as landslides and flooding. Every year, flash flooding inflicts extensive damage on sites sheltering internally displaced persons, and causes further displacement (for example, storm flooding in Lebanon in 2019) (UNHCR 2019c). It can also have indirect impacts on public health and water supplies because flooding often leads to stagnant water that becomes a breeding ground for disease vectors (such as dengue and cholera).

Unplanned Burden on Water Services in Host Communities

The sudden arrival of large numbers of forcibly displaced persons often causes severe stress on public services and environmental impacts on land, water, and other natural resources (World Bank 2017b). This can compound difficulties that some cities are already facing in providing basic services, including drinking water supply and wastewater collection and treatment services. The presence of forcibly displaced persons in host communities can also accelerate local phenomena of depletion of water resources and impact water quality. Countries of destination across the region are responding in different ways and to different extents to these challenges.

The arrival of Syrian refugees has amplified water challenges in Lebanon, in particular in relation to service delivery. Even before the Syrian crisis, Lebanon's water sector faced significant challenges, including inadequate technical, financial, and commercial performance (Bassil 2010). In particular, water supply service providers' struggle to meet basic household water needs has led to the development of a parallel off-network private water market, which accounted for 75 percent of total household water expenditure in 2010 (World Bank 2010). With the arrival of Syrian refugees, the volumetric demand for public water supplies has increased and with it the impact of unauthorized use, with estimates suggesting a 20 percent increase in domestic water use from the network (World Bank 2020b). The policy of Lebanon during the Syrian crisis has been, unlike that of Jordan, to refrain from allowing the setting up of formal refugee camps, which means that most refugees from Syria in the country are living in informal settlements, with lower water quality than in Palestinian refugee camps (see box 3.1). In informal settlements, water demands have been met through increasing reliance on boreholes for drinking water supplies, with water use from boreholes increasing fourfold compared with pre-crisis levels. Although boreholes have proved essential to meet increasing demand, their utilization affects affordability and quality because the water typically has to be trucked to informal settlements at a greater cost to users. Whereas Lebanon's water networks supply refugees hosted in residential buildings, the burden of supplying water to refugees in informal settlements is mostly shouldered by humanitarian agencies (nongovernmental organizations and United Nations entities) rather than national service providers.

Although the increase in population has led to increasing water consumption, this has not overall increased water stress in Lebanon.

Most water is consumed in the agricultural and industrial sectors, which withdraw about 700 million and 900 million cubic meters per year, respectively, according to Food and Agriculture Organization of the United Nations (FAO) Aquastat data. Therefore, refugee water use is a very minor share of total water use and has not led to large increases in water stress at the national level. At the local level, there are hot spots of increasing water stress, most notably in Baalbek, West Bekaa, and Zahle districts (Jaafar et al. 2020).

Jordan's well-known water scarcity issues, coupled with the influx of refugees, particularly in northern governorates, has increased pressure on existing water and sanitation systems (UNHCR 2019d). According to Jordan's Ministry of Planning and International Cooperation, annual water demand has increased by 40 percent in the northern governorates affected by the Syrian crisis and by 21 percent elsewhere in Jordan (Government of Jordan 2020). This situation underscores the need for Jordan to advance plans for water supply and wastewater treatment at a faster pace than originally planned. With the majority of refugees (around 80 percent) residing in host communities, increased focus is required on interventions and WASH improvements that serve both Jordanians and Syrians in vulnerable communities. Water is recognized as a key sector of concern in Jordan, with the government citing that the influx of refugees is creating new challenges in relation to deteriorating water quality and inadequate water supply because of increased demand. Jordanian government sources estimated the cost of providing water services to Syrian refugees to be around US$59 million in 2020 (Government of Jordan 2020). The Syrian refugee crisis has undoubtedly brought challenges to an already strained water sector, characterized by chronic water scarcity, unsustainable management, and aging and leaking infrastructure (Hussein et al. 2020).

Although host communities may face localized declines in water quality as more wastewater is generated through sudden influxes of refugees, there is no evidence of large-scale water pollution resulting from the Syrian crisis. For the three countries hosting most Syrian refugees (Iraq, Jordan, and Lebanon), no significant correlation exists between high refugee footprint and increasing levels of water pollution (World Bank 2020b), as shown in figure 3.12. There are no clusters of declining water quality corresponding to higher number of refugees in figure 3.12, suggesting that there is no clear signal at the country level. This is a correlational analysis, meaning that it is difficult to attribute the observed patterns to any specific policy intervention (such as host country adaptation) or preexisting conditions (for example, existing systems were capable of managing additional wastewater loads in some places). In addition, the locations with higher refugee concentration are more likely to experience an increase in pollution, especially in Iraq and Lebanon (points on the right side of the figure above the zero line), and also sewer overflows and blockages as a result of overloading of wastewater treatment plants, as reported in northern Jordan (Government of Jordan 2020).

FIGURE 3.12: Water Quality Trends and Number of Refugees in Iraq, Jordan, and Lebanon

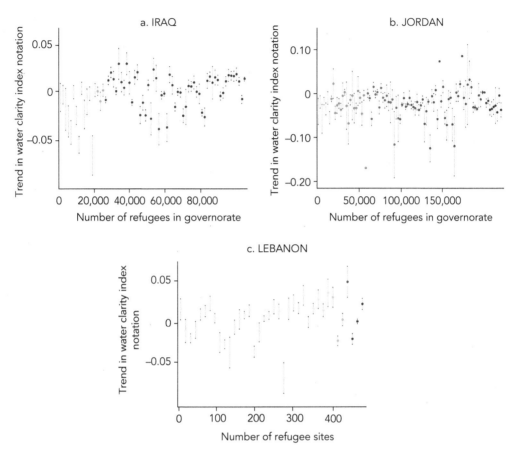

Source: World Bank 2020b.
Note: Dots present time trend estimates for each water site; vertical lines represent confidence intervals. The water sites are sorted from low refugee presence (left) to high refugee footprint (right). Positive slope coefficients (dots) where the standard error range does not overlap with zero indicate a significant and increasing pollution trend.

Host communities in Iraq have also faced water challenges in relation to the influx of Syrian refugees and IDPs. A large share of the forcibly displaced population is hosted in the Kurdistan region of Iraq, where there are at least 237,000 registered Syrian refugees and more than 1 million IDPs.[4] Together, this means that the population of the Kurdistan region of Iraq (Duhok, Erbil, Halabja, and Sulaymaniyah governorates) has increased by about 20 to 30 percent. Most refugees and IDPs live in host communities. By 2016, only a third of Syrian refugees and 20 percent of IDPs were still living in the 42 camps set up throughout the region (Saaid 2016). This influx of forcibly displaced persons led to increasing demand for services, affecting the provision of health, education, and social protection programs for the population in general (WHO 2019).

Perhaps surprisingly, water supply and sanitation coverage in the Kurdistan region of Iraq has slightly increased following the forcibly displaced persons crisis. This suggests that the region's government and its development partners adapted quickly to improve water supply, with indicators for coverage improving since the start of the Syrian crisis. In the Kurdistan region of Iraq, the proportion of households with access to piped water increased from 88 percent to more than 90 percent over the period.[5] For a selected number of utilities in the region with data, costs of production increased but so did revenues. As shown in figure 3.13, the resulting operating cost coverage ratio improved from 12 percent before the

FIGURE 3.13: Performance Data for Selected Utilities in Kurdistan Region of Iraq, 2011 and 2017

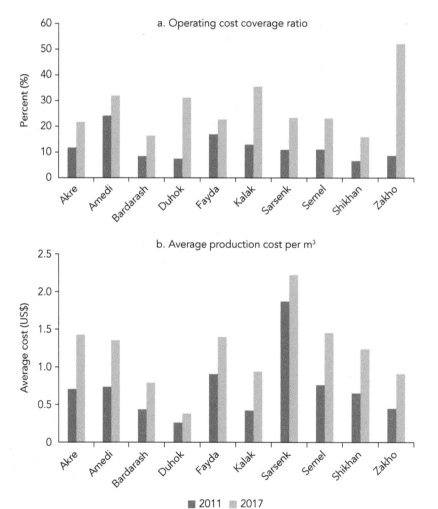

Source: World Bank based on IB-NET's country profile for Iraq.

crisis in 2011 to 27 percent in 2017. There may have been a modest fiscal impact on the regional government's budget and donors through additional capital investments for water projects and an estimated 10 percent increase in recurrent subsidies for water services.[6] Although sanitation coverage has slightly increased, this has not been accompanied by an increase in wastewater collection and treatment. As a result, most of the sewage across Iraq's cities in the Kurdistan region hosting IDPs and refugees is disposed of untreated, leading to deteriorating water quality for downstream communities.

COVID-19 EXACERBATES EXISTING VULNERABILITIES AND CREATES NEW CHALLENGES

Migrant populations are of particular concern for COVID-19, because of their vulnerability and potential to act as hubs of infection (Howard et al. 2020). At least three water-related challenges of forcibly displaced populations make water sanitation and hygiene a key concern for COVID-19 containment. First, camps have typically low environmental health and poor access to hygiene facilities and they are characterized by crowding, which leads to frequent interaction of households and individuals and makes containment largely ineffective. Second, water sources and sanitation facilities are often shared, providing opportunities for infection. Finally, in many camp settings, there is insufficient water for hand hygiene.

Access to drinking water among migrant populations has declined following the outbreak of the COVID-19 pandemic in some parts of the Middle East and North Africa. The disruptions to water and sanitation infrastructure make it more difficult for forcibly displaced persons and host communities to follow preventive protocols to reduce the spread of COVID-19. In September 2020, 25 percent of Libya's almost 600,000 international migrants reported having insufficient drinking water—more than twice the pre-COVID-19 proportion in January and February 2020 (11 percent) (IOM 2020b). This affects in particular unemployed migrants, with 38 percent of migrants reporting not having enough water to drink. In Jordan, Syrian refugees also reported having experienced declines in piped drinking water supplies and thus having increased their reliance on water tankers (box 3.4). Although they assist in the provision of water, excessive reliance on private water vendors can also create a situation in which these providers, as often happens in economies that are fragmenting during a conflict, have an indirect interest in the continued conflict. Those actors then risk becoming spoilers of peace, as is the case in other areas of Syria's war economy (Jazigi 2014; Gobat and Kostial 2016; Abboud 2017).

Although hygiene is critical for both containing the virus and lowering its immediate impact, it comes at a cost for vulnerable migrant households.

BOX 3.4: What Has COVID-19 Meant for Refugees' Water Security? Tales from Syrian Refugees in Jordan

To evaluate the impact of COVID-19 on refugees' water security, qualitative evidence from semistructured telephone interviews with 20 Syrian refugees living in camps and host communities in Jordan was collected. Respondents included Syrian male and female refugees living in the Zaatari camp and in host communities in Mafraq governorate, Amman, and ar-Ramtha. Respondents came from three cities in the Syrian Arab Republic (Dar'a, Homs, and Damascus), and they highlighted the conflict as the main reason for coming to their current location.

Across the four sites, respondents reported awareness of the importance of handwashing for containing and preventing the spread of COVID-19. Respondents also unanimously complained about increases in household expenditures resulting from the need to purchase hygiene kits. On average, households reported having to spend 10 Jordanian dinars more per month to purchase soap and hand sanitizers, with some households reporting expenses of as much as 20 to 40 Jordanian dinars per month. Given that the average monthly expenditures of refugee households in Jordan are reported to be in the range of 260–321 dinars (SIDA and UNHCR 2018; Tiltnes, Zhang, and Pedersen 2019), this poses a significant additional economic burden for many households.

In some instances, COVID-19 brought about additional challenges in relation to water supply. Two respondents in Mafraq reported having to buy water from water tankers because more frequent handwashing increased their household water consumption. Another respondent in Amman highlighted more frequent water supply network cuts, which led him to spend more to buy water from tankers. For a second respondent in Amman, water shortage and water outages led him to buy water from tankers, which constitutes an additional household expenditure. The cost of filling a 2-square-meter tank is 10 Jordanian dinars (around US$14).

Although COVID-19 has exacerbated some of the water and sanitation challenges faced by refugees, its impacts on livelihoods and incomes have been much larger. A female respondent, originally from Dar'a, Syria, described her life as "below zero." Because of the pandemic, she had lost her job, as had her husband, leaving them to rely on savings and borrowing. For another respondent, COVID-19 meant closing down his carpentry workshop, with decreasing revenue. "Fear of the unknown has once again taken over my life," he said. For some refugees, COVID-19 has altered future plans, forcing delays in pursuing education and even a life abroad. For others, however, COVID-19 seems not to have affected future prospects. One respondent had no future plans and just wanted to live safely and in good health, while another "lives day by day, whatever God plans for me I accept it," and did not perceive the pandemic as having changed his outlook on the future.

Source: World Bank based on qualitative semistructured interviews carried out by the West Asia-North Africa Institute for the World Bank Group.

For those living in substandard or crowded conditions—such as many IDPs, recent returnees, and migrants and refugees in the Middle East and North Africa's urban areas, camps, and detention centers—COVID-19 has led to an increased need for hygiene items (such as soap and alcohol-based hand rubs). However, high demand coupled with supply chain disruptions, especially at the outset of the pandemic, has led to price increases in many countries (UNOCHA 2020). Many vulnerable households have seen their expenditure on hand hygiene kits increase as a result. In Jordan, Syrian refugees highlighted increases in their expenditures to purchase soap and sanitizers (box 3.4).

CONCLUSIONS

The chapter demonstrates that water is a key determinant of vulnerability for forcibly displaced populations and host communities. For forcibly displaced persons, access to drinking water and sanitation is a key element of vulnerability, with millions across the region's conflict zones lacking everyday access to safe water. These challenges are particularly stark for some of the most vulnerable, such as persons with disabilities and women, for whom water insecurity has repercussions for mental well-being, exposure to violence, and marginalization. For host communities, the chapter describes the additional demands that forced displacement places on water service provision, notably drinking water supply and wastewater collection and treatment. Regional examples show that host communities can respond to these challenges and, indeed, have successfully done so, especially where local governance and institutions have adapted rapidly to the new conditions.

NOTES

1. Following UNRWA, Palestinian refugees are defined as "persons whose normal place of residence was Palestine during the period June 1, 1946, to May 15, 1948, and who lost both home and means of livelihood as a result of the 1948 conflict."
2. See https://www.who.int/teams/environment-climate-change-and-health/water -sanitation-and-health/environmental-health-in-emergencies/humanitarian -emergencies#minimum-quantity-water-needed.
3. A sufficient and adequate quantity of water means at least 15 liters of safe water (from improved water sources) per day.
4. Data from UNHCR's data portal: http://data2.unhcr.org/en/situations/syria/location/5.
5. World Bank data based on IB-NET's *Country Profile: Iraq* (https://database.ib-net .org/country_profile?ctry=143&years=2020,2019,2018,2017,2016&type=report&ent =country&mult=true&table=true&chart=false&chartType=column&lang=en&exch=1).
6. World Bank data based on IB-NET's *Country Profile: Iraq*. See website address in note 5 above.

REFERENCES

Abboud, S. 2017. "Social Change, Network Formation and Syria's War Economies." *Middle East Policy* 24 (1): 92–107.

Abu-Lohom, N. M., Y. Konishi, Y. Mumssen, B. Zabara, and S. M. Moore. 2018. *Water Supply in a War Zone.* Washington, DC: World Bank.

Arab Forum for the Rights of Persons with Disabilities. 2016. *Disability Inclusion among Refugees in the Middle East and North Africa: A Needs Assessment of Libya, Egypt, Yemen, Jordan, and Turkey.* http://www.disabledpeoplesinternational.org/documents/DPO-Report-FINAL.pdf.

Bassil, G. 2010. *National Water Sector Strategy.* Beirut, Lebanon: Ministry of Energy and Water.

CARE International. 2016. *On Her Own: How Women Forced to Flee from Syria Are Shouldering Increased Responsibility as They Struggle to Survive.* https://reliefweb.int/report/syrian-arab-republic/her-own-how-women-forced-flee-syria-are-shouldering-increased.

Doocy, S., and E. Lyles. 2017. "Humanitarian Needs among Displaced and Female-Headed Households in Government-Controlled Areas of Syria." *American Journal of Public Health* 107 (6): 950–59.

Gobat, J., and M. K. Kostial. 2016. *Syria's Conflict Economy.* International Monetary Fund.

Government of Jordan. 2020. *Jordan Response Plan for the Syria Crisis 2020–2022.* Beirut: Government of Jordan, Ministry of Planning and International Cooperation. http://www.jrp.gov.jo/Files/JRP%202020-2022%20web.pdf.

Habib, R. R., M. Ziadee, E. Abi Younes, H. Harastani, L. Hamdar, M. Jawad, and K. El Asmar. 2019. "Displacement, Deprivation and Hard Work among Syrian Refugee Children in Lebanon." *BMJ Global Health* 4 (1): e001122.

Haughton, J., and S. R. Khandker. 2009. *Handbook on Poverty and Inequality.* Washington, DC: World Bank.

Howard, G., J. Bartram, C. Brocklehurst, J. M. Colford Jr., F. Costa, D. Cunliffe, R. Dreibelbis, J. N. S. Eisenberg, B. Evans, R. Girones, S. Hrudey, J. Willetts, and C. Y. Wright. 2020. "COVID-19: Urgent Actions, Critical Reflections and Future Relevance of 'WaSH': Lessons for the Current and Future Pandemics." *Journal of Water and Health* 18 (5): 613–30.

Humanity & Inclusion and iMMAP. 2018. *Removing Barriers: The Path towards Inclusive Access. Disability Assessment among Syrian Refugees in Jordan and Lebanon: Jordan Report, July 2018.* Amman: Australian Aid, Humanity & Inclusion, and iMMAP. https://reliefweb.int/sites/reliefweb.int/files/resources/67818.pdf.

Hussein, H., A. Natta, A. A. K. Yehya, and B. Hamadna. 2020. "Syrian Refugees, Water Scarcity, and Dynamic Policies: How Do the New Refugee Discourses Impact Water Governance Debates in Lebanon and Jordan?" *Water* 12 (2): 325.

IDMC (Internal Displacement Monitoring Centre) and NRC (Norwegian Refugee Council). 2020. *Global Report on Internal Displacement.* Geneva: IDMC. https://www.internal-displacement.org/sites/default/files/publications/documents/2019-IDMC-GRID.pdf.

IOM (International Organization for Migration). 2019a. *IOM Displacement Tracking Matrix: Yemen Area Assessment, Round 37, March 2019.*

https://displacement.iom.int/system/tdf/reports/Yemen%20Area%20 Assessment%20Round%2037.pdf?file=1&type=node&id=5295.

IOM (International Organization for Migration). 2019b. *2018 Yemen: Multi-Cluster Location Assessment.* Geneva: IOM.

IOM (International Organization for Migration). 2019c. *Integrated Location Assessment IV.* https://displacement.iom.int/system/tdf/reports/20203124330549 _IOM%20-%20Integrated%20Location%20Assessment%20IV%20-%20 English%20-%20Digital.pdf?file=1&type=node&id=8104.

IOM (International Organization for Migration). 2020a. *Libya: IDP & Returnee Report, Round 32 (July–August 2020).* https://displacement.iom.int/reports /libya-—-idp-returnee-report-round-32-july-august-2020.

IOM (International Organization for Migration). 2020b. *Libya: Migrant Report 32 (July–August 2020).* https://migration.iom.int/reports/libya-%E2%80%94-migrant-report-32-july-august-2020.

Jaafar, H., F. Ahmad, L. Holtmeier, and C. King-Okumu. 2020. "Refugees, Water Balance, and Water Stress: Lessons Learned from Lebanon." *Ambio* 49 (6): 1179–93.

Yazigi, Y. 2014. "Syria's Water Economy." European Council of Foreign Relations policy brief.

Khoury, S., T. Graczyk, G. Burnham, M. Jurdi, and L. Goldman. 2016. "Drinking Water System Treatment and Contamination in Shatila Refugee Camp in Beirut, Lebanon." *Eastern Mediterranean Health Journal* 22 (8): 568–78.

Kuper, M., A. Hammani, A. Chohin, P. Garin, and M. Saaf. 2012. "When Groundwater Takes Over: Linking 40 Years of Agricultural and Groundwater Dynamics in a Large-Scale Irrigation Scheme in Morocco." *Irrigation and Drainage* 61: 45–53.

Masterson, A. R., J. Usta, J. Gupta, and A. S. Ettinger. 2014. "Assessment of Reproductive Health and Violence Against Women among Displaced Syrians in Lebanon." *BMC Women's Health* 14 (1): 1–8.

MSF (Médecins Sans Frontières). 2020. "In Al-Hol Camp, Almost No Healthcare Is Available." MSF, August 27, 2020. https://www.msf.org/covid -19-has-devastating-knock-effect-northeast-syria.

REACH. 2019. *WASH Situational Overview: Whole of Syria.* https://reliefweb .int/sites/reliefweb.int/files/resources/reach_syr_factsheet_wash_situational _overview_whole_of_syria_january_2019_0.pdf.

Saaid, H. M. 2016. "Syrian Refugees and the Kurdistan Region of Iraq." *Middle East Centre Blog.* The London School of Economics and Political Science.

SIDA and UNHCR. 2018. *Final Report: Assessing the Needs of Refugees for Financial and Non-Financial Services—Jordan.* https://www.unhcr.org /5bd01f7e4.pdf

Tiltnes, A., H. Zhang, and J. Pedersen. 2019. *The Living Conditions of Syrian Refugees in Jordan: Results from the 2017-2018 Survey of Syrian Refugees Inside and Outside Camps.* Fafo-report, 2019:04. https://reliefweb.int/sites /reliefweb.int/files/resources/67914.pdf.

UNEP (United Nations Environment Programme). 2020. *State of Environment and Outlook Report for the Occupied Palestinian Territory 2020.* https://www .unep.org/resources/report/state-environment-and-outlook-report-occupied -palestinian-territory-2020.

UNFPA (United Nations Population Fund). 2014. *Syrian Women-Headed Households: Hoping to Survive and Move On.* https://reliefweb.int/sites /reliefweb.int/files/resources/UNFPA%20Syrian%20women-%20 headed%20households%2C%20hoping%20to%20survive%20and%20 move%20on.pdf.

UNHCR (United Nations High Commissioner for Refugees). 2015. "Devastating Flooding Affects 25,000 Sahrawi Refugees in Tindouf Camps." UNHCR, October 23, 2015. https://www.unhcr.org/news/briefing /2015/10/562a19706/devastating-flooding-affects-25000-sahrawi-refugees -tindouf-camps.html.

UNHCR (United Nations High Commissioner for Refugees). 2016. *Humanitarian Needs of Sahrawi Refugees in Algeria 2016–2017.* Geneva: UNHCR. https://reporting.unhcr.org/sites/default/files/Humanitarian%20 Needs%20of%20Sahrawi%20Refugees%20in%20Algeria%202016 -2017%20-%20June%202016.pdf.

UNHCR (United Nations High Commissioner for Refugees). 2019a. *Power of Inclusion: Mapping the Protection Responses for Persons with Disabilities among Refugees in the Middle East and North Africa Region.* Geneva: UNHCR. https://www.unhcr.org/tr/wp-content/uploads/sites/14/2020/10/Power-of -Inclusion.pdf.

UNHCR (United Nations High Commissioner for Refugees). 2019b. *Vulnerability Assessment Framework: Population Study 2019.* https://data2.unhcr.org/en /documents/details/68856.

UNHCR (United Nations High Commissioner for Refugees). 2019c. "Storm Flooding Brings Misery to Syrian Refugees in Lebanon." UNHCR, January 11, 2019. https://www.unhcr.org/news/latest/2019/1/5c386d6d4/storm-flooding -brings-misery-syrian-refugees-lebanon.html.

UNHCR (United Nations High Commissioner for Refugees). 2019d. *WASH Q.4 Dashboard Report 2019: Jordan.* https://data2.unhcr.org/en/documents /details/73681.

UNHCR (United Nations High Commissioner for Refugees). 2020. "Fact Sheet: Yemen." UNHCR, Geneva. https://reporting.unhcr.org/sites/default /files/UNHCR%20Yemen%20Fact%20Sheet%20-%20August%202020 .pdf.

UNICEF (United Nations Children's Fund). 2020. "Eight Children Die in Al-Hol Camp, Northeastern Syria in Less Than a Week." Statement by UNICEF Executive Director Henrietta Fore, August 12, 2020. https://www.unicef.org /press-releases/eight-children-die-al-hol-camp-northeastern-syria-less-week.

United Nations and Partners. 2016. *Humanitarian Responses for Syrian Refugees in Jordan: Inter-Agency Task Force (IATF) WASH Sector Gender Analysis in Za'atari and Azraq Refugee Camp.* https://reliefweb.int/sites /reliefweb.int/files/resources/WASHSectorGenderAnalysisinZa%27atariand Azraqcamps%282016%29%5B1%5D.pdf.

UNOCHA (United Nations Office for the Coordination of Humanitarian Affairs). 2019b. *2019 Humanitarian Needs Review: Syrian Arab Republic.* https://reliefweb.int/report/syrian-arab-republic/2019-humanitarian-needs -overview-syrian-arab-republic-enar.

UNOCHA (United Nations Office for the Coordination of Humanitarian Affairs). 2019a. *Humanitarian Needs Overview: Iraq.* https://reliefweb.int /report/iraq/iraq-humanitarian-needs-overview-2019-november-2018.

UNOCHA (United Nations Office for the Coordination of Humanitarian Affairs). 2020. *2020 Humanitarian Response Monitoring: Periodic Monitoring Report (Jan-May 2020) Libya.* https://reliefweb.int/sites/reliefweb.int/files /resources/libya_hrp_2020_pmr.pdf.

UNRWA (United Nations Relief and Works Agency for Palestine Refugees in the Near East). 2019. *Annual Operational Report 2019.* https://www.unrwa .org/sites/default/files/content/resources/aor_2019_eng.pdf.

UN Women. 2020. *Gender Alert: Needs of Women, Girls, Boys and Men in Humanitarian Action in Palestine.* UN Women Palestine Country Office. https://www2.unwomen.org/-/media/field%20office%20palestine /attachments/publications/2020/10/gender%20alert%20analysis%20 august%202020%20unw.pdf?la=en&vs=5731.

USAID (United States Agency for International Development). 2020. "Water, Sanitation, and Hygiene Fact Sheet." https://www.usaid.gov/sites/default /files/documents/1883/USAID_Yemen_WASH_Fact_Sheet_March_2020 .pdf.

Vivar, M., N. Pichel, M. Fuentes, and F. Martínez. 2016. "An Insight into the Drinking-Water Access in the Health Institutions at the Saharawi Refugee Camps in Tindouf (Algeria) after 40 Years of Conflict." *Science of the Total Environment* 550: 534–46.

WFP (World Food Programme). 2018. *Gender, Risks and Urban Livelihoods Study in Three Cities in Syria: Aleppo, Homs, and Lattakia.* https://www.wfp .org/publications/gender-risks-and-urban-livelihoods-study-three-cities -syria-aleppo-homs-and-lattakia.

WHO (World Health Organization). 2019. "WHO Providing Health Care to Syrian Refugees in and outside the Camps." WHO Regional Office for the Eastern Mediterranean.

WHO (World Health Organization) and UNICEF (United Nations Children's Fund). 2016. *Lebanon Water Quality Survey.* https://www.unicef.org/lebanon /media/576/file/JMP%20Report.pdf.

WHO (World Health Organization) and World Bank. 2011. *World Report on Disability.* Geneva: World Health Organization. https://www.who.int /publications/i/item/9789241564182.

World Bank. 2010. *Republic of Lebanon. Water Sector: Public Expenditure Review.* Washington, DC: World Bank.

World Bank. 2017a. *Cities of Refuge in the Middle East: Bringing an Urban Lens to the Forced Displacement Challenge.* Washington, DC: World Bank.

World Bank. 2017b. *Dire Straits: The Crisis Surrounding Poverty, Conflict, and Water in the Republic of Yemen.* Washington, DC: World Bank.

World Bank. 2018a. *Avenues for Social and Economic Inclusion in Livelihoods in West Bank and Gaza* (English). Washington, DC: World Bank. http:// documents.worldbank.org/curated/en/627191554487756315/Avenues-for -Social-and-Economic-Inclusion-in-Livelihoods-in-West-Bank-and-Gaza.

World Bank. 2018b. *Toward Water Security for Palestinians.* Washington, DC: World Bank. https://ideas.repec.org/p/wbk/wboper/30316.html.

World Bank. 2020a. *Convergence: Five Critical Steps toward Integrating Lagging and Leading Areas in the Middle East and North Africa.* Washington, DC: World Bank.

World Bank. 2020b. *The Fallout of War: The Regional Consequences of the Conflict in Syria.* Washington, DC: World Bank.

World Bank. 2020c. *The Mobility of Displaced Syrians: An Economic and Social Analysis.* Washington, DC: World Bank.

CHAPTER FOUR

WATER: AN OPPORTUNITY FOR PROTECTING THE MOST VULNERABLE AND BUILDING RESILIENCE

KEY HIGHLIGHTS

- The reality of protracted forced displacement requires a shift from humanitarian support toward a development approach for water security, including a structured yet flexible master planning vision to deliver water services and to sustain water resources for forcibly displaced populations and their host communities.

- Closer coordination between actors (security, humanitarian, and development) in situations of protracted crisis is imperative, including from pre-crisis, to onset of conflict, during the conflict phase, as well as in the post-conflict phase, allowing for improved approaches whereby actors can build on the work of others.

- When working toward this coordination, policy makers will likely face trade-offs between short-term uncoordinated measures to respond to immediate water needs and long-term measures needed to address structural water sector issues. Failure to recognize and manage these trade-offs can significantly undermine water security prospects for forcibly displaced populations and their host communities.

- Policies to reconstruct national water institutions and infrastructure are likely to fail without the foundations of a renewed social fabric and trust in institutions, which can be achieved through people- and area-based interventions.

INTRODUCTION

The preceding chapters have shown that water risks exacerbate the vulnerabilities of forcibly displaced populations and host communities in the Middle East and North Africa. Rather than trying to unpack complex causal links between water, forced displacement, and conflict, the preceding chapters suggest that development policy and analysis should focus on designing interventions to address the water risks faced by forcibly displaced people and host communities now and in the future. The region's forced displacement situation is protracted, meaning that there is an urgent need to develop and implement sustainable, long-term solutions to enhance water security and build resilience to future shocks. This is even more urgent in light of the COVID-19 (coronavirus) pandemic, which has made addressing some of these risks more difficult, especially for countries and people already facing difficult circumstances. The poverty impact of COVID-19 and ensuing confinement policies have increased humanitarian needs across the region (World Bank-UNHCR Joint Data Centre 2020). Responses commensurate with the magnitude of the vulnerabilities described in the previous chapters are needed to prevent further misery and sliding into water insecurity.

Designing and operationalizing interventions to this end is difficult and requires innovative approaches to financing and implementation, especially in contexts characterized by protracted armed conflict. As expressed in the World Bank Group's *Strategy for Fragility, Conflict, and Violence 2020–2025*, promoting development interventions in these contexts means pursuing synergies between humanitarian, security, and development responses (World Bank 2020d). Development agencies and governments increasingly work with humanitarian and security actors to reduce vulnerabilities to shocks and to meet the immediate needs of forcibly displaced populations and host communities, with the goal of supporting human development and poverty eradication efforts without undermining long-term prospects for sustainable peace (United Nations and World Bank 2018; World Bank, ICRC, and UNICEF 2021).

During recent decades, there has been an increasing realization that the old model in which different international actors intervene and provide support during various phases of a conflict is largely outdated, both because conflicts are more protracted and because conflict rarely moves neatly through phases. On the contrary, the conflict dynamic tends to be fluid, and to consider it as a continuum is often unhelpful. Efforts by the World Bank and key humanitarian actors, such as the United Nations Children's Fund (UNICEF) and the

International Committee of the Red Cross (ICRC), to find a partnership model in which humanitarian and development efforts can be increasingly aligned have been ramped up during recent years. These partnerships are intended to be transformational rather than transactional and therefore require sustained attention and a genuine willingness to adapt to achieve the changes needed (World Bank, ICRC, and UNICEF 2021). In the context of the World Bank's changing approach to engagement in fragile contexts, this chapter explores how water sector interventions, and development actors in particular, can respond to the challenge of forced displacement.

FROM PEOPLE'S GRIEVANCES TO REGIONAL DYNAMICS: AN INTEGRATED FRAMEWORK TO RESPOND TO WATER RISKS DURING PROTRACTED FORCED DISPLACEMENT

As other World Bank studies on the Middle East and North Africa have shown (World Bank 2020b, 2020c), responding to the region's protracted forced displacement crisis requires an integrated approach that takes into consideration people, the places where they live and operate, and regional power dynamics. At the most basic level, considering people's incentives and location is essential because forced displacement and conflict conditions might vary within a country or region, requiring careful analysis of the local context. However, this is not enough, as certain water risks (such as flood risks in a transboundary river basin) might be better managed and resolved at the regional level. Hence, an integrated approach also allows development actors to consider regional perspectives (figure 4.1).

The components of figure 4.1 should be understood as building blocks to enhance water security for forcibly displaced populations and their host communities in the Middle East and North Africa. This is a context characterized by high levels of forced displacement and complex water sector issues. As highlighted in the Introduction, water sector issues include, but are not limited to, unsustainable levels of water use; high levels of spatial inequality in water service provision between rural and urban areas; and long-standing (almost half a century in some cases) issues regarding water risks for marginalized people. In situations of active conflict, it will be impossible to address some of these structural sector issues. However, development actors should remain engaged to support the work of humanitarian and security actors through, for example, data collection and sharing and capital injections, as shown in figure 4.1.

In situations of development, people- and area-based interventions constitute the first building block toward water security. Policies to reconstruct national institutions and components of water resource management are likely to fail without the foundations of a renewed social

FIGURE 4.1: Approach for Development Actors to Promote Water Security for Forcibly Displaced People and Their Host Communities

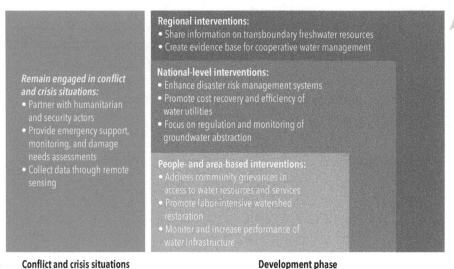

Regional interventions:
• Share information on transboundary freshwater resources
• Create evidence base for cooperative water management

National-level interventions:
• Enhance disaster risk management systems
• Promote cost recovery and efficiency of water utilities
• Focus on regulation and monitoring of groundwater abstraction

People- and area-based interventions:
• Address community grievances in access to water resources and services
• Promote labor-intensive watershed restoration
• Monitor and increase performance of water infrastructure

Remain engaged in conflict and crisis situations:
• Partner with humanitarian and security actors
• Provide emergency support, monitoring, and damage needs assessments
• Collect data through remote sensing

Spatial scale

Conflict and crisis situations

Development phase

Source: World Bank.

fabric and trust in institutions, which can be achieved through people- and area-based interventions. Likewise, regional efforts toward water security are much harder to deliver if individual countries do not have the institutions and capacity to manage water resources and are not prepared to confront water extremes, such as floods and droughts. Hence, figure 4.1 suggests that water policies to address complex forced displacement and conflict challenges should start from people- and area-based approaches and then gradually move toward greater scales of interventions.

People- and area-based approaches can help to address grievances and social inclusion barriers—notably gender gaps—related to access to water resources and services in protracted crisis situations. Grievances over water access can act as barriers to state-building and can contribute to fragility, as discussed in chapter 2. Carefully designed people- and area-based interventions focus on people's most pressing needs in the context of legacies of violence, disrupted economic and social networks, and grievances, as also shown by World Bank experiences in Uganda (box 4.1). By adopting this approach, water sector interventions can contribute to broader efforts aimed at mending the destroyed socioeconomic fabric of the region's communities affected by conflict and forced displacement (World Bank 2020a).

In the water sector, people- and area-based interventions focus on ensuring access to water services and protecting livelihood opportunities that are supported by water. Public work programs to reverse the degradation of watersheds and other labor-intensive approaches to monitor, clean up, and restore degraded water resources enhance water's potential to support livelihoods (see box 4.2

BOX 4.1: Bridging Humanitarian Response and Development in Uganda: The Integrated Water Management and Development Project

With more than 1.4 million refugees, Uganda is the largest refugee host country in Africa and the fourth largest refugee host country in the world. To face this protracted forced displacement crisis, Uganda has adopted one of the most progressive refugee policies in the world that allows refugees to move freely and gain access to public services and gives them the right to work. Nonetheless, the sheer number of refugees puts exceptional constraints on the country's capacity to deliver effective water services to refugee populations and host communities. In the upper West Nile region, where about 60 percent of the refugees are hosted, the lack of inclusive access to clean water and sanitation, and of water for livelihoods, negatively affects human capital development and climate resilience for both refugees and host communities.

Humanitarian partners have stepped in to ensure that lives are saved and public health risks are minimized through water trucking and rapid construction of water schemes across refugee settlements. Although these responses provide much-needed emergency relief, they are carried out with minimal coordination among the partners; as a result, most water systems are transient in nature, of substandard quality, and plagued by operational inefficiencies and high operating costs. This type of provision of water services to refugees is fragmented and unsustainable because of perpetual institutional constraints and financing gaps. In addition, failure to consider equity dimensions and potential conflicts between refugees and host communities over water access further undermines the long-term sustainability of some of these solutions.

The government of Uganda has been working with the World Bank and the United Nations High Commissioner for Refugees to explore alternative water delivery models to improve the sustainability of service provision to refugees and hosting areas. Through the World Bank-financed Integrated Water Management and Development Project, refugees are being integrated into the national development agenda and water system planning, and the provision of water services is being shifted from humanitarian partners to Uganda's national utility (National Water and Sewerage Corporation). This project is helping to harmonize infrastructure development across partners, and to improve the capacity of the Ministry of Water and Environment and the national utility to plan adaptable water systems and consider issues faced by host communities as well as refugees in accessing water services. The project also demonstrates the critical role of technical assistance and analytics in shaping policy reform to face context- and community-specific water security challenges in the context of forced displacement

Source: World Bank data based on research by Ai-Ju Huang, Fook Chuan Eng, and Alexander Danilenko.

BOX 4.2: Emerging Lessons from the Development Response to Displacement Impacts Project in the Horn of Africa

The Horn of Africa faces a refugee crisis of staggering proportions. Conflict, drought, and persecution have driven more than 4 million of the world's most vulnerable people from their homes (World Bank 2020c). The region currently hosts an estimated 20 percent of the global refugee population. Within host countries, refugees often reside in historically underserved border areas that are also environmentally fragile. This places additional strain on communities already facing a precarious socioeconomic situation plagued by food insecurity, limited access to basic social services and economic infrastructure, poor livelihood opportunities, and a degraded natural resource base.

The Development Response to Displacement Impacts Project addresses the challenges in areas hosting refugees through an innovative design and implementation approach. Funded by the World Bank, the project is a government-led and community-driven project focusing on the impact of the protracted presence of refugees on host communities in four countries: Djibouti (US$20 million, US$10 million under preparation), Ethiopia (US$100 million), Uganda (US$200 million), and Kenya (US$100 million and US$8.18 million from the Danish government).

The project has three aspects of relevance to humanitarian–development interventions in the Middle East and North Africa:

- **Focus on underresourced marginalized areas with highly depleted natural capital.** The environmental management plan of the Development Response to Displacement Impacts Project has focused on rehabilitation of degraded lands. Interventions followed the watershed approach, which included community plans, development of base maps, needs identification, prioritization, and multiyear plans and execution. This approach has contributed to watershed and forest restoration and target development of small irrigation systems.

- **Adopt an area-based approach and empower local governments.** The project uses an area-based planning approach that enables local communities to identify and prioritize investments. Currently, there are established committees representing both refugees and host communities that meet regularly, discuss outstanding issues, resolve problems, devise solutions jointly, and monitor progress. The local government-based approach promotes and improves the use of government systems—government financing systems, governance structure, and institutions—for delivering a development response to forced displacement, thus strengthening government institutions.

box continues next page

BOX 4.2: **Emerging Lessons from the Development Response to Displacement Impacts Project in the Horn of Africa** *continued*

- **Employ a community-driven development approach.** This involves (a) building and capacitating grassroots institutions; (b) ensuring that the voice of all communities is heard in decision making; (c) strengthening decentralized government administrative functions; and (d) investing in public service delivery and social mobilization to enhance social cohesion among beneficiary communities.

The project demonstrates that water resource management activities can be used as a vehicle to pursue both social cohesion and water security objectives. The project's dual focus on enhancing natural resource management, including halting depletion of freshwater resources, and on area-based planning is a case in point. The project undertakes targeted at-scale community-based watershed restoration, which (a) helps capture rainwater through labor-intensive public works and (b) integrates host and refugee communities.

Source: IGAD 2020; World Bank 2020d.

for a discussion of the World Bank's experience in the Horn of Africa). These interventions can be ways of creating jobs and boosting economic growth while restoring environmental services and natural capital (Barbier 2010). Investing in the preservation or restoration of watersheds that provide resilience against floods and droughts can boost shorter-term job creation while also providing long-term benefits. Providing stimulus to public work programs that employ thousands of people to generate valuable assets that focus on irrigation and drainage schemes and watershed development can help provide a more reliable water supply in the years to come (Subbarao et al. 2013). In the Republic of Korea, for example, the multipurpose Four Major Rivers Restoration Project is estimated to have created 340,000 jobs from 2009 to 2013, improving the quality of water and ecosystems in the target river basins while reducing drought and flood risks (Ishiwatari et al. 2016).

People-based interventions can also support activities to empower and build the skills of those who are responsible for water resource management and supplies within forcibly displaced and host communities. In Lebanon, for example, the World Bank's Lebanon Municipal Services Emergency Project targeted both the host community and Syrian refugees (World Bank 2014). The project used a decentralized and consultative approach to promote women's inclusion and ensure that women's voices were heard when decisions were made about the selection of water infrastructure alternatives for the community. For example, to address the specific issue of water-related infections and diseases, the project held consultations with community groups and included consultations in smaller community settings (Hanmer et al. 2019). It reached out to groups that were especially vulnerable, including youths, the elderly, and refugee populations, and in particular it reached out to the women in these groups because they are chiefly responsible for domestic water supplies.

When conditions allow, building the skills of forcibly displaced persons in controlled environment agriculture might also be an option to enhance water and food security. Many of the Middle East and North Africa's forcibly displaced persons have backgrounds in agriculture (Verner et al. 2017). Shukreyeh, a Syrian refugee in Jordan interviewed as part of this study, was a farmer before the civil war broke out, and now she often wishes she had more water for her plants in Jordan. Agricultural interventions centered around water-saving agricultural production or controlled environment agriculture provide opportunities to improve the livelihoods, skills, and mental health of forcibly displaced persons (box 4.3).

People-based interventions require careful consideration of people's incentives and priorities. In Jordan, host communities' interest in expanding and increasing the value of their properties has been matched with the need to provide long-term housing solutions for refugees. Jordanian homeowners have been offered financing to enlarge their houses in exchange for hosting Syrian refugees. This mechanism effectively subsidizes improvements in housing that benefit homeowners (through increased property value) and refugees (through long-term access to housing and basic services, including water and sanitation) (NRC 2014).

People- and area-based interventions need to be aligned with investments in national-level institutions and infrastructure. These interventions aim at restoring the national-level building blocks that are essential to ensure sustainable water management and service delivery. Institutional interventions can focus on groundwater management and regulation, as well as financial sustainability issues for service providers. Institutional responses also need to consider policy levers outside the water sector. For example, land zoning and housing policies to prevent displaced communities from settling in areas prone to floods (such as wadis) or with depleted or difficult-to-access water sources can ensure long-term sustainability. Similarly, an increased focus on the nexus between land rights, informal settlements, and water service provision can help legislators identify ways to ensure that concerns over land ownership and long-term presence of settlements do not prevent improvements in water services from being realized. Beyond land policy, agricultural and energy subsidies, social protection, and trade policy all have fundamental roles in enabling or hindering the impacts of water policy, and hence have to be considered when developing responses to complex water security challenges at the national level.

Water infrastructure is often a target of conflict. Hence, investments in water infrastructure not only need to focus on restoring or upgrading water services, but also they need to plan for the repeated targeting of this

BOX 4.3: Controlled Environment Agriculture for Forcibly Displaced Populations and Host Communities

Controlled environment agriculture offers one way of increasing food production and supporting livelihoods in the land- and water-scarce Middle East and North Africa. Controlled environment agriculture typically adopts hydroponics, a method of growing plants using a nutrient solution, which is a mixture of water and nutrient salts, without the presence of soil in greenhouses or buildings. Hydroponic systems use approximately 80–99 percent less water than open field agriculture, thus having minimal water and land footprints while resulting in higher yields (Despommier 2010). However, these systems typically have much higher energy consumption than conventional methods, making them particularly attractive for water-scarce settings with abundant renewable energy potential, such as the Middle East and North Africa (Barbosa et al. 2015).

Hydroponic systems require trained labor, suggesting that their implementation needs to go hand in hand with agricultural extension services to enhance skills and human capital. Examples from Jordan, the West Bank and Gaza, and the United Arab Emirates show that the required skills and techniques can be rapidly acquired by people with little formal education (Verner et al. 2017). In sum, hydroponics provides access to nutritious food, improves livelihoods and jobs, and builds human capital with minimal land and water footprint. These three characteristics make it an attractive option to enhance food security and livelihood opportunities for forcibly displaced people in the region, who also typically face severe nutrition deficiencies. Furthermore, gardening and nurturing plants can also positively affect mental health and trauma recovery in forcibly displaced populations (Millican, Perkins, and Adam-Bradford 2018). Forcibly displaced persons in the region are already growing vegetables through hydroponics, highlighting opportunities to implement these projects at scale. In Gaza, hydroponics has been piloted since 2010 to provide livelihood opportunities and additional food sources to food-insecure households (Verner et al. 2017).

same infrastructure (Weinthal and Sowers 2019). Mitigating the impacts of conflict on water services and infrastructure requires more attention to infrastructure planning issues, so that new investments are designed to be resilient in the face of potential targeting. In practice, this means that infrastructure designs should all have built-in redundancy (replicating elements of infrastructure, designing systems with diversified supply sources) and contingency plans (stocking up consumables for water treatment plants, nominating replacement staff) (Zeitoun and Talhami 2016). It also means investing in wastewater treatment infrastructure that is easier to operate and maintain, such as stabilization ponds and wetlands, whose functioning is less dependent on electricity and customized mechanical parts, which are often not available in times of crisis.

Finally, a political economy approach that considers a regional perspective complements the national-level and people- and area-based approaches. As has been noted by earlier work (World Bank 2020b), a regional approach in recovery from crisis is preferable over a unilateral approach. The Syrian conflict, for example, has led to a number of regional externalities, not just in terms of the tragic numbers of forcibly displaced people, but also in terms of a decrease in cross-border trade. These are examples of "public bads" that require a concerted regional (and international) effort to be overcome. Transboundary waters offer another example of cross-border flows and regional issues whose public good benefits can turn into public bads without a concerted effort by regional actors. Transboundary water management represents a regional public good with benefits beyond the national realm (Nicol et al. 2001). Actors promoting a regional perspective can support capacity building on transboundary water management, increased data and information sharing, and the pursuit of cooperative agreements. With more than 60 percent of the region's water resources being transboundary, and with climate change adding further pressure on already scarce resources, support to improve the management of transboundary waters represents a concrete way in which development and diplomatic actors can contribute to water security for forcibly displaced people and their host communities. This support includes providing evidence-based analysis outlining key reasons for countries to cooperate (Sadoff and Grey 2005), and providing platforms for countries to interact, build trust, and support the sharing of data and information, including the use of disruptive technologies.

THE PATH NOT TAKEN: TRADE-OFFS BETWEEN SHORT-TERM GAINS AND LONG-TERM SUSTAINABILITY SHAPE SUCCESS

The previous section introduced an overall approach to water sector interventions in contexts affected by protracted forced displacement. When working toward this approach, policy makers will likely face trade-offs between short-term uncoordinated measures to respond to immediate water needs and long-*term* measures needed to address structural water sector issues. These trade-offs are time specific, meaning that they can create path dependencies and lock-in, thus influencing countries' ability to achieve water security over the long term. Hence, at different stages of a protracted forced displacement crisis, policy makers need to be cognizant that their efforts can undermine or support long-term water security objectives.

Figure 4.2a shows three decision points at which specific trade-offs shape which paths are taken in sending and receiving regions. The structure of figure 4.2a resembles a decision tree: policy makers confront a series of

FIGURE 4.2: Decision Points, Pathways, and Water Security Outcomes for Forcibly Displaced People and their Host Communities

a. Decision Points and Pathways to Water Security for Forcibly Displaced People and their Host Communities

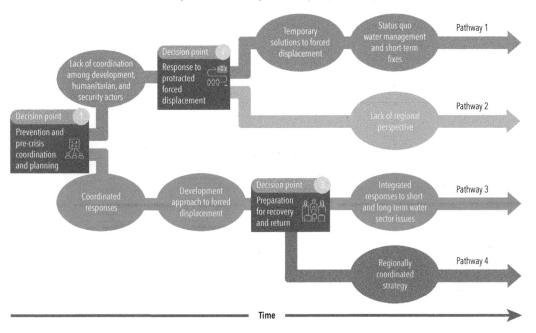

b. Water Security Outcomes for Forcibly Displaced People and their Host Communities Under Alternative Pathways

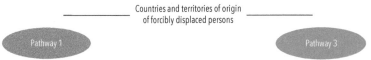

Countries and territories of origin of forcibly displaced persons

Pathway 1

Status quo water management leaves immediate needs unaddressed while factional interests undermine water resource base and crowd out public water service providers:

• Water sector interventions reinforce grievances and discrimination
• Encroachment of water resources by factional interests

Pathway 3

Integrated responses help forcibly displaced persons overcome immediate needs while addressing structural water sector issues:

• Continued monitoring of water risks and vulnerabilities of forcibly displaced persons
• People- and area-based approaches address grievances in access to water resources and services
• Capacity of water sector institutions to regulate and monitor water use is strengthened, staff are trained in environmental peacebuilding
• Reestablishment of damaged water infrastructure considers resilience criteria and repeated targeting

Countries and territories hosting forcibly displaced persons

Pathway 2

Temporary solutions to forced displacement and limited regional coordination exacerbate water risks in host countries and heightens risk of tensions among communities.

Pathway 4

Regionally coordinated strategy helps identify scale and location of long-term water sector responses to forced displacement and reduces tensions with host communities and risk of infrastructure targeting.

Source: World Bank.

choices through time (from left to right) and their choice will determine the type of outcomes they are able to achieve. While timing and responses will be context specific, these decision points are likely to arise in any protracted forced displacement situation, making this framework generally applicable across the Middle East and North Africa and beyond. For each of these decision points, policy makers need to explore trade-offs between addressing short-term needs and achieving more longer-term solutions.

Decision point 1: Prevention and pre-crisis coordination and planning. Coordination among development, humanitarian, and security actors helps build preparedness in fragile situations. Development actors have access to ministries and service providers and should ensure that these public sector entities that are tasked with managing water and delivering services establish functional links with humanitarian and security actors (World Bank, ICRC, and UNICEF 2021). In addition, development actors should promote and support data collection and information-sharing protocols to build a common understanding across parties involved in water management in fragile contexts. A joint understanding of water resource availability and safe deployable outputs (that is, the quantity of water that can be consumed without compromising it through depletion or salinization) and of water governance structures can ensure that humanitarian actors have a better understanding when water resources might be compromised or depleted during a crisis. This joint understanding also involves mapping critical interconnected infrastructure systems, notably energy, digital, and water infrastructure, and ensuring that there are no single points of failure which—if targeted—can bring down the entire system.

Decision point 2: Response to protracted forced displacement. During a protracted forced displacement crisis, policy makers in the country of origin face significant trade-offs between short-term responses to meet immediate needs and long-term measures that address underlying sector weaknesses. Overreliance on private sector service providers can undermine long-term institutional ability to provide sector oversight and deliver services in the long run. Private water vendors might be interested in maintaining control of water distribution even after the crisis ends, complicating the transition to a sustainable and affordable water delivery model. They might also not be interested in protecting water sources from pollution and overexploitation or in promoting drilling of new wells, contributing to an uncontrolled expansion of unlicensed users (figure 4.2b, pathway 1). Hence, a longer-term view that supports business continuity of water service providers and water resource management agencies with one-off capital injections helps to ensure sustainability in the long term.

Although sustainability of use and resource protection might not seem priorities in the short term, they are key tenets of a development approach to the forced displacement crisis. Often, short-term responses, such as drilling a well, can have long-term impacts on the sustainability of both short- and long-term interventions by inevitably depleting or contaminating water resources. Hence, a development approach helps to rationalize the use of existing water resources and prioritize demand-side solutions (for example, reducing water use) to avoid placing additional pressures on already strained supplies, and the use of integrated gray and green solutions to respond to flood risks (figure 4.2b, pathway 3).

Decision point 3: Preparation for recovery and return. A development approach to the water security of forcibly displaced populations in the host countries is dependent on a range of integrated measures. Water sector investments are integrated within broader plans to extend basic services to camps and informal settlements, rehabilitate irrigation canals, and expand the capacity of existing urban water systems to respond to higher demand (figure 4.2b, pathway 3). For example, a higher presence of refugees in urban areas can increase demand (as shown in chapter 3), highlighting the need to upgrade and in some cases increase the capacity of existing supply and sanitation infrastructure. These increases in demand are different from normal surges in demand for water services, which are typically short-lived increases in demand in response to weather conditions or public health measures (for example, COVID-19 lockdowns). In contrast to these demand surges, forced displacement causes long-lasting increases in service demand, thus requiring a master plan and long-term response. For water utilities and service providers, restoring and expanding services will be an opportunity to improve service quality for their own constituents and customers while avoiding promotion of exclusionary practices that benefit factional interests and that can contribute to fragility (Sadoff, Borgomeo, and de Waal 2017).

A development approach to forced displacement in the host countries should also consider a regional perspective (figure 4.2a, pathway 4). Following a protracted forced displacement crisis, new economic realities and incentives might arise. In some situations, the forcibly displaced populations might not intend to go back to their place of origin (as reported by many Syrian refugees; see IPA 2020). In this case, it might make more economic sense for development actors to prioritize the use of scarce financial resources to support the expansion of water infrastructure in the host country rather than to rebuild infrastructure in the place of origin. A regional perspective also helps to identify opportunities to share benefits from transboundary waters and identify regionally beneficial approaches to water management.

Although a development approach grounded in regional considerations helps to address water sector issues in host countries, it might be challenging to adopt in practice. In already politically fragile and financially stretched contexts, host country governments might not be willing or able to provide water services to forcibly displaced communities (figure 4.2a, pathway 2). In turn, this leaves humanitarian actors or unregulated private vendors to meet the immediate needs of vulnerable populations. However, these short-term responses might be counterproductive in the long run because they might create patterns of inclusion and exclusion between host communities and forcibly displaced populations, making integration and cohesion harder to achieve. When host communities perceive that forcibly displaced populations are receiving better services through humanitarian actors, this can fuel grievances against the forcibly displaced populations and the state. While temporary solutions might offer a relatively easier way to respond to forced displacement, they can also lead to lock-in and foreclose alternatives in the long term for host countries. The different responses to the Syrian refugee crisis observed in Jordan, Lebanon, and Turkey demonstrate this problem: the water security of forcibly displaced populations and their host communities varies significantly depending on host countries' willingness and ability to adopt a long-term development approach to the crisis rather than short-term temporary solutions (see chapter 3).

REFERENCES

Barbier, E. B. 2010. *A Global Green New Deal: Rethinking the Economic Recovery.* Cambridge: Cambridge University Press.

Barbosa, G. L., F. D. A. Gadelha, N. Kublik, A. Proctor, L. Reichelm, E. Weissinger, M. Gregory, M. Wohlleb, and R. U. Halden. 2015. "Comparison of Land, Water, and Energy Requirements of Lettuce Grown Using Hydroponic vs. Conventional Agricultural Methods." *International Journal of Environmental Research and Public Health* 12 (6): 6879–91.

Despommier, D. 2010. *The Vertical Farm: Feeding the World in the 21st Century.* New York: Macmillan.

Hanmer, L., D. Arango, J. Damboeck, E. Rubiano, and D. Villacres. 2019. *Addressing the Needs of Women and Girls in Contexts of Forced Displacement: Experiences from Operations.* Washington, DC: World Bank.

IGAD (Intergovernmental Authority on Development). 2020. "A Development Approach to Forced Displacement: Emerging Lessons from Early Practices." Policy brief. https://regionaldss.org/wp-content/uploads/2020/01/Highlights-of -DRDIP-for-GRF.pdf.

IPA (Innovations for Poverty Action). 2020. "Returning Home? Conditions in Syria, Not Lebanon, Drive the Return Intentions of Syrian Refugees." Policy brief. https://www.poverty-action.org/publication/returning-home-conditions -syria-not-lebanon-drive-return-intentions-syrian-refugees.

Ishiwatari, M., E. Wataya, T. Shin, D. Kim, J. Song, and S. Kim. 2016. *Promoting Green Growth through Water Resources Management: The Case of Republic of Korea* (English). Green Growth in Action Knowledge Note Series, No. 3. World Bank, Washington, DC.

Millican, J., C. Perkins, and A. Adam-Bradford. 2018. "Gardening in Displacement: The Benefits of Cultivating in Crisis." *Journal of Refugee Studies* 32 (3): 351–71.

Nicol, A., F. van Steenbergen, H. Sunman, T. Turton, T. Slaymaker, T. Allan, M. de Graaf, and M. van Harten. 2001. *Transboundary Water Management as an International Public Good.* Stockholm, Sweden: Ministry of Foreign Affairs.

NRC (Norwegian Refugee Council). 2014. *Shared Resilience for Syrian Refugees and Host Communities in Jordan.* https://reliefweb.int/sites/reliefweb.int/files /resources/nrc_jordan_case_study_web.pdf.

Sadoff, C. W., E. Borgomeo, and D. de Waal. 2017. *Turbulent Waters: Pursuing Water Security in Fragile Contexts.* Washington, DC: World Bank.

Sadoff, C. W., and D. Grey. 2005. "Cooperation on International Rivers: A Continuum for Securing and Sharing Benefits." *Water International* 30 (4): 420–27.

Subbarao, K., C. del Ninno, C. Andrews, and C. Rodríguez-Alas. 2013. *Public Works as a Safety Net: Design, Evidence, and Implementation.* Directions in Development. Washington, DC: World Bank.

United Nations and World Bank. 2018. *Pathways for Peace: Inclusive Approaches to Preventing Violent Conflict.* Washington, DC: World Bank.

Verner, D., S. Vellani, A. L. Klausen, and E. Tebaldi. 2017. *Frontier Agriculture for Improving Refugee Livelihoods: Unleashing Climate-Smart and Water-Saving Agriculture Technologies in MENA.* Washington, DC: World Bank.

Weinthal, E., and J. Sowers. 2019. "Targeting Infrastructure and Livelihoods in the West Bank and Gaza." *International Affairs* 95 (2): 319–40.

World Bank. 2014. *Lebanon: Municipal Services Emergency Project* (English). Washington, DC: World Bank.

World Bank. 2020a. *Building for Peace: Reconstruction for Security, Equity, and Sustainable Peace in MENA.* Washington, DC: World Bank.

World Bank. 2020b. *The Fallout of War: The Regional Consequences of the Conflict in Syria.* Washington, DC: World Bank.

World Bank. 2020c. *From Isolation to Integration: The Borderlands of the Horn of Africa.* Washington, DC: World Bank.

World Bank. 2020d. *World Bank Group Strategy for Fragility, Conflict, and Violence 2020–2025* (English). Washington, DC: World Bank.

World Bank, ICRC (International Committee of the Red Cross), and UNICEF (United Nations Children's Fund). 2021. *Joining Forces to Combat Protracted Crises: Humanitarian and Development Support for Water and Sanitation Providers in the Middle East and North Africa.* Washington, DC: World Bank.

World Bank--UNHCR (United Nations High Commissioner for Refugees) Joint Data Centre. 2020. *Compounding Misfortunes: Changes in Poverty Since the Onset of COVID-19 on Syrian Refugees and Host Communities in Jordan, the Kurdistan Region of Iraq and Lebanon.* Washington, DC: World Bank.

Zeitoun, M., and M. Talhami. 2016. "The Impact of Explosive Weapons on Urban Services: Direct and Reverberating Effects across Space and Time." *International Review of the Red Cross* 98 (1): 53–70.

DEFINITIONS OF SELECTED TERMS USED IN THIS REPORT

In accordance with the International Organization for Migration's *Glossary on Migration* (IOM 2019), this report defines these terms as follows:

- *Asylum seeker*—an individual who is seeking international protection. In countries with individualized procedures, an asylum seeker is someone whose claim has not yet been finally decided on by the country in which he or she has submitted it. Not every asylum seeker will ultimately be recognized as a refugee, but every recognized refugee is initially an asylum seeker.

- *Internally displaced persons*—persons or groups of persons who have been forced or obliged to flee or to leave their homes or places of habitual residence, in particular as a result of or to avoid the effects of armed conflict, situations of generalized violence, violations of human rights, or natural or human-made disasters, and who have not crossed an internationally recognized state border.

- *Migrant*—a person who moves away from his or her place of usual residence, whether within a country or across an international border, temporarily or permanently, and for a variety of reasons. This term includes categories of people who are well-defined under international law, such as refugees or smuggled migrants, but also individuals whose status is not recognized under international law (for example, internally displaced persons).

- *Refugee* (1951 Refugee Convention)—a person who, owing to a well-founded fear of persecution for reasons of race, religion, nationality, or membership of a particular social group or political opinion, is outside the country of his or her nationality and is unable or, owing to such fear, is unwilling to avail himself or herself of the protection of that country; or who, not having a nationality and being outside the country of his or her former habitual residence as a result of such events, is unable or, owing to such fear, is unwilling to return to it.

In addition, per the United Nations Relief and Works Agency for Palestine Refugees in the Near East (UNRWA), *Palestinian refugees* are defined as "persons whose normal place of residence was Palestine during the period June 1, 1946 to May 15, 1948, and who lost both home and means of livelihood as a result of the 1948 conflict" (UNRWA 2021).

REFERENCES

IOM (International Organization for Migration). 2019. *Glossary on Migration.* Geneva: IOM. https://www.iom.int/glossary-migration-2019.

UNRWA (United Nations Relief and Works Agency for Palestine Refugees in the Near East). 2021. "Palestine Refugees." UNRWA, Amman. https://www.unrwa.org/palestine-refugees.

WATER CONFLICT AND COOPERATION EVENT DATA SETS

INTRODUCTION

Conflict studies in recent years have increasingly employed national and subnational event data sets to examine causes and consequences of conflict (Ide 2018; Bernauer and Böhmelt 2020; Döring 2020). This report, and in particular chapter 2, follows this approach and relies extensively on event databases to study the relationship between water and conflict in the Middle East and North Africa. While both data sets used in this study have been vetted and widely used in the academic and policy literature, it is important to acknowledge their limitations and carry out additional tests to assess if these limitations have any major impact on the result. This appendix presents additional results from two of the event data sets used in this report and demonstrates that overall findings are robust to alternative ways of curating the data sets.

WATER-RELATED INTRASTATE CONFLICT AND COOPERATION DATABASE

Limitations exist in the Water-Related Intrastate Conflict and Cooperation (WARICC) database,[1] warranting some data curation and examination of subsets of the full sample to ensure that overall results are consistent and coherent despite these limitations. First, a large share of events in this database are georeferenced to capital cities because events for which geolocation data were not available were assigned to capital cities (Bernauer et al. 2012). This higher number of events located in cities is also likely due to greater presence and coverage of news agencies in capital cities. Many of the events coded are based on journalistic reports, which are often produced in capital cities. Finally, embassies are typically located in capital cities and typically tend to be involved in cooperative interactions. To examine whether events in capital cities significantly skewed the overall distribution and types of events, a sample of cooperative and conflictive events located outside capital cities only was created and analyzed.

A second problem with the WARICC database arises through potential reporting bias and attention to specific conflicts and regions within the Middle East and North Africa. As noted earlier, many of the events coded in the WARICC database build at least partially on journalistic reports, which tend to focus on some of the region's well-known crises, notably the Israeli-Palestinian conflict. To avoid potential reporting bias toward this specific conflict and any impact it might have on the frequency of cooperative versus conflictive events, a sample excluding all events located in Israel and West Bank and Gaza was generated, with and without capital cities.

Two additional tests were carried out to ensure overall consistency of the results. First, event frequency for North Africa and the Levant was examined to check for any subregional patterns. Second, events involving United Nations agencies, regional cooperation agencies (such as the Arab League), donors (such as the United States Agency for International Development), and development banks (such as the World Bank and the Islamic Development Bank) were removed from the data set. These events are overwhelmingly cooperative because of the actors involved and their missions, and thus

Table B.1: Number of Events Recorded in the WARICC Data Set by Event Type for Different Samples of the Full Data Set

	All events, full data set	Events outside capital cities	Events NOT located in Israel and/ or West Bank and Gaza	Events outside capital cities and NOT located in Israel and/ or West Bank and Gaza	Events in North Africa only	Events in the Levant only	Events NOT involving international agencies, donors, and development banks
Number of conflictive events (%)	641 (21%)	389 (30%)	317 (16%)	242 (18%)	172 (16%)	469 (23%)	259 (19%)
Number of cooperative events (%)	864 (28%)	327 (25%)	680 (33%)	452 (35%)	378 (36%)	486 (24%)	438 (33%)
Number of neutral events (%)	1,603 (52%)	601 (46%)	1,033 (51%)	616 (47%)	514 (48%)	1,089 (53%)	632 (48%)
Total	3,108	1,317	2,030	1,310	1,064	2,044	1,329

Source: World Bank using data from Bernauer et al. 2012.
Note: WARICC = Water-Related Intrastate Conflict and Cooperation.

removing them allows to account for any potential skewing effect they might have on the frequency of cooperative events. Across all subsamples, cooperative events occur more frequently than conflictive events, confirming the overall finding that according to this database water is more often a source of cooperation than conflict within countries (table B.1).

TRANSBOUNDARY FRESHWATER DISPUTE DATABASE

The Transboundary Freshwater Dispute database[2] from Oregon State University was used to detect trends in international events relating to water (table B.2). The full data set was filtered to remove all entries in which at least one country was not located in the Middle East and North Africa. Events reporting interactions happening between a country in the Middle East and North Africa and a country outside the Middle East and North Africa were retained because they might indicate interactions on transboundary rivers with riparians located outside the region (for example, the Nile and the Tigris-Euphrates). The records were further filtered to remove interactions in which at least one Middle East and North Africa country was involved but in which the river basin in question was located outside the region (for example, the Arab Republic of Egypt hosting riparians of the Congo River basin for talks). These were further filtered by event type to remove any event not directly involving international waterways as a consumable resource or quantity to be managed (for example, navigation, shipping, borders). In addition, all events tagged as research were removed from the analysis because this tag implies that further research needs to be undertaken before that entry can be properly classified. This leaves a total of 975 events, which were used to estimate the frequency of cooperative and conflictive events reported in chapter 2.

As discussed for the WARICC database, the data from the Transboundary Freshwater Dispute database also has some limitations. Contrary to the WARICC database, this database is not georeferenced (that is, entries do not have coordinates), thus effectively removing the issue of event clustering in cities. However, this data set is also largely built from media and news reports, which are likely to focus on some of the more well-known regional conflicts and rivers (for example, the Israeli-Palestinian conflict), and likely to overlook other less-known basins. To test for these potential effects, the data set was divided into subsets to check for any changes in the frequency of occurrence of cooperative and conflictive events. First, all events involving Israel and West Bank and Gaza were removed because they tend to receive more media coverage and thus are likely to be overrepresented in the database. Second, all events that involved water, but not as a consumable good or quantity (for example, navigation, border issues, sea access), were reincorporated in the sample. Finally, all events recorded as being strictly

Table B.2: Countries Involved and Number of Events Recorded in the Transboundary Freshwater Dispute Database by Event Type for Different Samples of the Full Data Set

Event type	Events involving an international basin that involves nation(s) that are riparian and/or not riparian to that basin, in which water is involved as either a consumable resource or a quantity to be managed	Events between riparian nations concerning an international basin that they share, in which water is involved as either a consumable resource or a quantity to be managed		All event types			
Countries involved	All, including riparians outside MENA	All, including riparians outside MENA	Only riparians inside MENA	All, excluding Israel and West Bank and Gaza	All, including riparians outside MENA	All, including events involving river basins outside MENA but involving MENA countries	All, including riparians outside MENA, 2000–08
Number of conflictive events (%)	356 (37%)	289 (42%)	227 (43%)	248 (30%)	430 (36%)	464 (31%)	18 (29%)
Number of cooperative events (%)	544 (56%)	336 (49%)	261 (50%)	521 (63%)	676 (57%)	918 (62%)	43 (68%)
Number of neutral events (%)	75 (8%)	62 (9%)	38 (7%)	59 (7%)	86 (7%)	92 (6%)	2 (3%)
Total	**975**	**687**	**526**	**828**	**1,192**	**1,474**	**63**

Source: World Bank analysis using data from the Transboundary Freshwater Dispute database, Oregon State University.
Note: All data for 1948–2000 except where noted. "All event types" includes events between nations concerning an international river basin in which water is involved not only as a consumable resource or quantity but also for navigation, shipping, or territory issues. For a full list of event types included in the database see Oregon State University 2017. MENA = Middle East and North Africa.

occurring among riparians of an international basin in the region were analyzed. Those events are entries in the database marked as an event between riparian nations concerning an international basin that they share, in which water is involved as either a consumable resource or a quantity to be managed (Oregon State University 2017). Across all subsamples, cooperation occurs more frequently than conflict.

NOTES

1. The WARICC database is available at https://www.prio.org/Publications/Publication /?x=5118.
2. The Transboundary Freshwater Dispute database is available at https://transboundarywaters.science.oregonstate.edu/content/international-water -event-database.

REFERENCES

Bernauer, T., and T. Böhmelt. 2020. "International Conflict and Cooperation over Freshwater Resources." *Nature Sustainability* 3 (5): 350–56.

Bernauer, T., T. Böhmelt, H. Buhaug, N. P. Gleditsch, T. Tribaldos, E. B. Weibust, and G. Wischnath. 2012. "Water-Related Intrastate Conflict and Cooperation (WARICC): A New Event Dataset." *International Interactions: Empirical and Theoretical Research in International Relations* 38 (4): 529–45.

Döring, S. 2020. "From Bullets to Boreholes: A Disaggregated Analysis of Domestic Water Cooperation in Drought-Prone Regions." *Global Environmental Change* 65: 102147.

Ide, T. 2018. "Climate War in the Middle East? Drought, the Syrian Civil War and the State of Climate-Conflict Research." *Current Climate Change Reports* 4 (4): 347–54.

Oregon State University. 2017. *Appendix 1. Field Descriptions for Event Database.* https://transboundarywaters.science.oregonstate.edu/sites/transboundarywaters .science.oregonstate.edu/files/Database/ResearchProjects/BAR/BAR_appendices .pdf.

INTERVIEWS WITH KEY INFORMANTS

OVERVIEW

To shed light on some of the dynamics of water, migration, and conflict in the region, 18 key informants from different countries and backgrounds, including researchers, experts, professors, and technical engineers, were interviewed as part of this study. The interviews were administered by the West Asia-North Africa (WANA) Institute. WANA also transcribed recordings of each interview and prepared interview summaries.

Semistructured interviews were conducted both in person and virtually. Each key informant was asked a set of qualitative questions on water, conflict, and migration in the Middle East and North Africa region that pertained to his or her knowledge area. In addition, key informants who expressed interest participated in an expert elicitation that focused on three themes, detailed in box C.1.

All key informants agreed to WANA's consent form for participation in research interviews. Anonymity and confidentiality in the aggregated findings were ensured through the use of randomized key informant codes (table C.1).

Table C.1: Key Informants Interviewed as Part of This Study

Key informant code	Group	Country	Date of interview
KI-1	Water and energy security regional expert, Middle East and North Africa region	Jordan, Netherlands	June 15, 2020
KI-2[a]	Research fellow, international relations and water diplomacy, Middle East and North Africa region	United Kingdom	June 15, 2020
KI-3[a]	Water resources management expert, Mediterranean countries	Italy	June 16, 2020
KI-4[a]	Agriculture and irrigation expert	Tunisia	June 18, 2020
KI-5[a]	Adviser, water and conflict	Netherlands	June 18, 2020
KI-6[a]	International relations expert	United States	July 1, 2020
KI-7[a]	Energy expert	Jordan	June 22, 2020
KI-8[a]	Water and geological expert	Jordan	June 23, 2020
KI-9	Geopolitical expert	Jordan	June 24, 2020
KI-10[a]	Food security expert	Lebanon	July 1, 2020
KI-11[a]	Water infrastructure specialist in refugee camps	Jordan, Lebanon	June 15, 2020
KI-12	Hydrology and water resources expert	United Kingdom	June 15, 2020
KI-13	WASH specialist	Jordan	June 23, 2020
KI-14	Water expert	Tunisia	July 16, 2020
KI-15	Host community	Jordan	July 19, 2020
KI-16	Host community	Jordan	July 19, 2020
KI-17	Host community	Jordan	July 19, 2020
KI-18	Journalist specializing in water issues	Iraq	July 29, 2020

Note: WASH = water, sanitation, and hygiene.
a. Expert who agreed to take part in the expert elicitation study.

EXPERT ELICITATION

Expert elicitation is a well-vetted interview method from the applied decision and policy analysis sciences. The interviews conducted for this report centered on three themes (box C.1). This approach is based on a recent global expert elicitation on similar topics (Mach et al. 2019).

BOX C.1: Expert Elicitation Themes and Questions in Key Informant Questionnaire

Theme 1. Relative Importance and Uncertainty of Causal Factors Driving Migration

- Rank the five most important factors driving migration in the Middle East and North Africa. [1 most important, 5 less important]
- Rank the five factors for which you believe there is the most uncertainty about their influence on migration. [1 most uncertain, 5 less uncertain]

- High crime
- High temperatures
- Pollution
- High risk from natural hazards (floods, earthquakes, dust storms)
- Lack of fertile land
- Lack of services
- Lack of education opportunities
- Lack of water access
- Conflict in neighboring areas

- History of violence
- Crop failure/drought
- Economic shocks (e.g., international financial crisis)
- Corruption
- Lack of employment opportunities
- War

Theme 2. Relative Importance and Uncertainty of Causal Factors Driving Conflict

- Rank the five most important factors driving armed conflict in the Middle East and North Africa. [1 most important, 5 less important]
- Rank the five factors for which you believe there is the most uncertainty about their influence on armed conflict. [1 most uncertain, 5 less uncertain]

- Climate change-induced water shocks (floods, droughts)
- Economic shocks (e.g., international financial crisis)
- Population pressure
- Low state capacity
- Income inequality
- Illiberal governments

- Unemployment
- Corruption
- Natural resource dependency (livelihoods depend on natural resources)
- Conflict in neighboring areas
- Mistrust of government
- External intervention

Theme 3. Relationship between Climate and Migration at Present and in the Future

Across the Middle East and North Africa examples of forced migration, do you think that water shocks led to substantial, moderate, or negligible changes in migration rates? Please tick one option.

Substantial ☐   Moderate ☐   Negligible ☐

box continues next page

BOX C.1: Expert Elicitation Themes and Questions in Key Informant Questionnaire *continued*

Under future climate change, do you think water shocks will lead to substantial, moderate, or negligible changes in migration rates? Assume no adaptation. Please tick one option.

Substantial ☐   Moderate ☐   Negligible ☐

How much is a potential relationship between water issues and migration important to the decisions and choices made by national governments, civil society organizations, or international donors? Please tick one option.

Substantial ☐   Moderate ☐   Negligible ☐

REFERENCE

Mach, K. J., C. M. Kraan, W. N. Adger, H. Buhaug, M. Burke, J. D. Fearon, C. B. Field, C. S. Hendrix, J. F. Maystadt, J. O'Loughlin, and P. Roessler. 2019. "Climate as a Risk Factor for Armed Conflict." *Nature* 571 (7764): 193–97.

INTERVIEWS WITH REFUGEES IN JORDAN AND LEBANON

To explore the effect of migration on both country of destination and country of origin from a community angle, interviews were conducted with 21 refugees in two of the biggest camps in the Middle East and North Africa region. This research included 10 interviews conducted at the Zaatari camp in Jordan and 11 interviews conducted at the Shatila camp in Lebanon.

The interviews were administered by the West Asia-North Africa (WANA) Institute. WANA also transcribed recordings of each interview and prepared interview summaries. The interviews were conducted in person and over the phone. All interviewees agreed to WANA's consent form for participation in research interviews. Anonymity and confidentiality in the aggregated findings were ensured through the use of randomized key informant codes.

Included in chapter 3 are real-life stories from refugees living in camp settings: one narrative zooms in on a day in the life of a refugee living in the Zaatari camp; another narrative provides the story behind the establishment of the Shatila camp. These sample narratives do not represent all residents of the Shatila and Zaatari camps; however, their opinions are used to study attitudes among forcibly displaced persons in these areas.

In addition, in October 2020, WANA administered a questionnaire to 20 Syrian refugees living in four areas in Jordan (Amman, Mafraq, Ramtha, and Zaatari) to document their vulnerabilities in relation to water security and the COVID-19 pandemic (box D.1).

BOX D.1: Topics and Questions on Impacts of COVID-19 and Water Security Questionnaire

Context and Existing Vulnerabilities

Current conditions and context:
- When did you arrive?
- Did you arrive on your own or with relatives?
- Are there relatives or village members residing in the same camp or nearby host community?
- Why did you leave the Syrian Arab Republic?

Perception of water risks:
- Are you concerned by the risk of flooding in Jordan?
- Are you concerned by the risk of water shortage?
- Was water shortage a concern in Syria?

General Perceptions around Welfare, Safety, and Mobility

Do you know anyone around you who has had COVID-19 or knows someone who has had COVID-19? [*In this question, ensure no personal reference is made to avoid stigma or fear of being linked with COVID-19*]

Has the COVID-19 pandemic affected you directly? [*Response: very much, partially, very little*]

If answer is "very much" or "partially," please explain how. For example:
- Forced to change economic activity or job
- Received lower remittances
- Increased mental stress due to health concerns/risk of contagion
- Restricted mobility

Has the COVID-19 pandemic affected plans for next year? For example:
- Returning home
- Finding a job
- Moving outside the camp into host community

Hand Hygiene and WASH (Water, Sanitation, and Hygiene)

Are you aware of the importance of handwashing in preventing COVID-19? [*Yes/no; if answer is yes, ask the following:*]
- Has the need to ensure hand hygiene increased your expenditure on hand hygiene kits (soap)?

box continues next page

BOX D.1: Topics and Questions on Impacts of COVID-19 and Water Security Questionnaire *continued*

Has your water consumption changed? [*Please mention the following aspects and ask if they are occurring:*]
- Use more bottled water
- Changes to the water fetching routine
- Higher cost of water from tankers
- More frequent handwashing means less water for plants/laundry

Has COVID-19 brought about additional challenges to life in the camp and to getting water?

What is your typical water source? Has this source changed following the COVID-19 pandemic?

Coping Mechanisms and Perception of Responses

- Have you adapted your daily routine to cope with the impact of COVID-19? If yes, how?
- To what extent are the actions undertaken by authorities of your host country (or camp authorities) in this pandemic period helping you? [*Response: very much, partially, not at all*]
- Have any awareness plans been done in camp on COVID-19 (importance of washing, etc.) or do you just know from social media outlets (TV, radio, or online)?